HOME REPAIR AND IMPROVEMENT

DECKS, PORCHES, AND PATIOS

TIME®
LIFE
BOOKS

Other Publications
JOURNEY THROUGH THE MIND AND BODY
WEIGHT WATCHERS® SMART CHOICE RECIPE COLLECTION
TRUE CRIME
THE AMERICAN INDIANS
THE ART OF WOODWORKING
LOST CIVILIZATIONS
ECHOES OF GLORY
THE NEW FACE OF WAR
HOW THINGS WORK
WINGS OF WAR
CREATIVE EVERYDAY COOKING
COLLECTOR'S LIBRARY OF THE UNKNOWN
CLASSICS OF WORLD WAR II
TIME-LIFE LIBRARY OF CURIOUS AND UNUSUAL FACTS
AMERICAN COUNTRY
VOYAGE THROUGH THE UNIVERSE
THE THIRD REICH
THE TIME-LIFE GARDENER'S GUIDE
MYSTERIES OF THE UNKNOWN
TIME FRAME
FIX IT YOURSELF
FITNESS, HEALTH & NUTRITION
SUCCESSFUL PARENTING
HEALTHY HOME COOKING
UNDERSTANDING COMPUTERS
LIBRARY OF NATIONS
THE ENCHANTED WORLD
THE KODAK LIBRARY OF CREATIVE PHOTOGRAPHY
GREAT MEALS IN MINUTES
THE CIVIL WAR
PLANET EARTH
COLLECTOR'S LIBRARY OF THE CIVIL WAR
THE EPIC OF FLIGHT
THE GOOD COOK
WORLD WAR II
THE OLD WEST

For information on and a full description
of any of the Time-Life Books series listed above,
please call 1-800-621-7026 or write:
Reader Information
Time-Life Customer Service
P.O. Box C-32068
Richmond, Virginia 23261-2068

HOME REPAIR AND IMPROVEMENT

DECKS, PORCHES, AND PATIOS

BY THE EDITORS OF TIME-LIFE BOOKS, ALEXANDRIA, VIRGINIA

The Consultants

Mark M. Steele is a professional home inspector in the Washington, D.C., area. He has developed and conducted training programs in home-ownership skills for first-time homeowners. He appears frequently on television and radio as an expert in home repair and other consumer topics.

Jeff Palumbo is a registered journeyman carpenter who has a home-building and remodeling business in northern Virginia. His interest in carpentry was sparked by his grandfather, a master carpenter with more than 50 years experience. Mr. Palumbo teaches in the Fairfax County Adult Education program.

J. Paul Trueblood consults and teaches in the civil engineering field. He served in the U.S. Marine Corps as a civil engineer for 25 years before retiring in 1983.

CONTENTS

1

Repairs and Refurbishments

After years of service, even the sturdiest deck, porch, or patio may need a measure of restoration. Screens are damaged with surprising ease. Wooden structures eventually begin to deteriorate even if built of rot-resistant lumber, and concrete may crack, admitting water that can crumble a patio. Timely repairs can prevent irreparable damage and assure continued durability— and even safety—of valued outdoor amenities.

Although they are tough and durable, screens are often accidentally torn or punctured. Holes up to a few inches across can be patched with the technique shown below, but repairing greater damage—or deterioration from age—requires a new panel of mesh.

Types of Mesh: Replacement screening comes in a variety of widths and mesh sizes in lengths up to 100 feet. Standard widths are 24, 36, 48, 60, and 72 inches. The most common mesh size is 16 by 18. Having 16 horizontal filaments per inch and 18 per inch vertically, this mesh is fine enough to keep out most flies and mosquitoes.

Among screening materials, fiberglass and aluminum are the most popular. Aluminum is the more durable choice, but fiberglass is less expensive, is available in more colors, and comes in a densely woven variety called solar screening. This type of mesh blocks up to two-thirds of the sun's rays, making it a good choice for southern and western exposures.

Wood Frames or Aluminum: To replace screening on a wood frame, you'll need shears to cut the mesh, a stiff putty knife to pry molding off the frame, and a staple gun loaded with $\frac{3}{8}$-inch copper-coated staples. If the frame is rotten or broken, build a new one *(page 10)*. To do so you will need a miter box and backsaw to cut the frame pieces, as well as corner clamps to hold the pieces for nailing. To install mesh in an aluminum frame, buy several feet of vinyl cord called screen spline and a tool called a screen-spline roller.

Covering a hole.
◆ Cut a piece of matching screening about twice as large as the opening.
◆ For aluminum screening, fold opposite sides of the patch to 90° angles, about $\frac{1}{2}$ inch from the edges, as shown at right. Then detach wires to make a fringe *(inset)*.
◆ Pass the wires through the screen mesh around the hole and fold them against the screen to hold the patch in place.
◆ For fiberglass screening, sew the patch around the edges with nylon monofilament thread.

SCREEN-SPLINE ROLLER

SPLINE

New screen for an aluminum frame.
◆ Remove damaged screening by pulling the flexible vinyl spline out of the channel around the edge, and cut a new piece of screening that overlaps the spline channel by 1 inch on each side.
◆ If you are using aluminum screening, crease it into the channel with a screen-spline roller. *(Skip this step with fiberglass screening.)*
◆ Position a length of new spline over the screening at one end of the frame, and roll the spline and screening into the channel. Trim away excess spline at the corners.
◆ Repeat this procedure at the opposite end and then along the sides, pulling the screen tight as you work. When finished, trim the screen along the outer edge of the spline.

Rescreening a wood frame.

◆ Pry off the molding that covers the screen edges and remove the old screening.

◆ Clamp the middle of the frame to boards laid across sawhorses or other supports and push narrow shims under each corner so that the frame is slightly bowed *(right)*.

◆ Unroll the screening over the frame, overlapping the ends of the frame by at least 1 inch. Starting at one corner, staple the screening to one end of the frame at 2-inch intervals, $\frac{1}{2}$ inch from the inside edge of the frame.

◆ Pull the screening to remove wrinkles and staple it across the other end. Next, remove the shims and staple the screen to the sides, corner to corner,

then use a utility knife to trim the edges about $\frac{1}{2}$ inch from the staples.

◆ If the molding is sound, reinstall it; otherwise, cut new molding *(page 10, Step 1)*.

Support for a sagging door.

To stop a screen door from scraping a porch floor or patio as it opens and closes, true the door with a wire-and-turnbuckle stay.

◆ Open a 3-inch turnbuckle to its full extension, and attach a 4-foot length of woven wire to each of its eyes with a wire clamp *(inset)*.

◆ Drive $\frac{1}{2}$-inch screw eyes into the corners of the door as shown above and clamp the free ends of the turnbuckle wires to them. Trim excess wire.

◆ Using pliers if needed, tighten the turnbuckle to restore the door to a rectangular shape.

ASSEMBLING A FRAME FOR A SCREEN

1. Mitering the frame corners.
Using a backsaw and miter box, cut each end of four 1-by-2s at a 45° angle as shown above. Make the long edge of each piece $\frac{1}{4}$ inch shorter than the corresponding edge of the opening for the screen.

2. Joining the pieces.
◆ Secure two adjacent sides of the frame in a corner clamp, then remove one of the sides and apply glue to the end. Reposition it in the clamp.
◆ Drill two $\frac{1}{16}$-inch pilot holes into the corner (above) and drive a 2-inch finishing nail into each. Repeat this procedure to join the other three corners.
◆ Staple screening to the frame (page 9).

3. Adding the molding.
Cover the staples with $1\frac{3}{8}$-by-$\frac{1}{4}$-inch lattice strips, mitered to match the frame pieces. Align the outer edges of the lattice strips with the outer edges of the frame, and fasten them with $\frac{3}{4}$-inch brads driven near each edge at 6-inch intervals.

The major causes of damage to porches and decks are rot and insects. Spongy, discolored wood indicates rot; piles of wood fibers or detached wings signal insect activity. If insects are present, exterminate them before trying any repairs.

Widespread damage may require replacing the entire structure, but in most cases, the affected parts can simply be repaired or replaced. With the exception of porch flooring, which is usually protected by weather-resistant paint, make all repairs with pressure-treated lumber to prevent rot and galvanized nails and hardware to prevent rust.

Using a Jack: Before replacing a post or a column, support the structure above with a screw-operated, telescoping jack. Use a bell jack—a strong, bell-shaped screw jack about 1 foot tall—under a low deck or porch. Before using either type, grease the threads so the jack will operate smoothly.

Periodic Checks: After the repair has been completed, a little routine maintenance can prevent further trouble. If the porch or deck is painted, scrape clean and repaint any blisters or cracked areas as soon as they appear. If the structure is not painted, treat it once a year with a wood preservative. And regular inspections for rot and insect damage will catch any problems before they become severe.

⚠️ **CAUTION** *Do not use a hydraulic jack; the weight of a porch or deck may gradually compress the jack.*

SAFETY TIPS *Protect your eyes when hammering nails and when using a circular saw. Wearing earplugs reduces the noise of this tool to a safe level. Wearing a dust mask is advisable when sawing pressure-treated lumber, which contains arsenic compounds as preservatives. And be sure to wash your hands thoroughly after handling pressure-treated wood. Finally, wear a hard hat when handling heavy objects overhead.*

PATCHING A TONGUE-AND-GROOVE FLOOR

1. Chiseling floorboards.
With a 1-inch wood chisel, chip deep grooves across each damaged floorboard on both sides of the damage.
◆ Center the chisel on a joist, with the tool's beveled edge facing the damage. Drive the chisel straight down to cut deep across the board.
◆ Reverse the chisel, move it about ½ inch closer to the damaged area, then drive it toward the first cut, chipping out a groove.
◆ Repeat for each damaged board, staggering the grooves so that adjacent boards are not cut over the same joist.

2. Removing the boards.
◆ With a circular saw set to the thickness of the floorboards, make two parallel cuts down the middle of every damaged board that is longer than damaged boards next to it. Start and stop the saw just short of the chiseled ends, and complete the cuts with a wood chisel.
◆ Use a pry bar to remove first the middle strip, then the tongued side, and finally the grooved side of each board. The remaining boards can be pried out without sawing.

3. Inserting new boards.

◆ Where no floorboard blocks the way, tap a replacement into position with a rubber mallet, fitting the grooved edge over the tongue of the undamaged board next to it.

◆ Drive a $2\frac{1}{2}$-inch finishing nail through the corner of its tongue into the joists below *(inset)*.

◆ Fit as many boards as possible this way. For any pieces that cannot be wedged into place, use the alternative method described in Step 4.

4. Installing the final boards.

◆ Where a neighboring floorboard hinders fitting a replacement, chisel off the lower lip of the new board's grooved edge. Place its tongue in the groove of the adjacent board, and drop its trimmed edge into place *(inset)*, tapping it gently with a rubber mallet to seat it.

◆ Nail the board at each joist with two $2\frac{1}{2}$-inch finishing nails, set at an angle to minimize shifting of the board. Countersink the nails and fill the holes with wood putty.

STRENGTHENING JOISTS

Reinforcing a joist.

To strengthen a weak joist, fit a new joist alongside the existing one, as shown above.

◆ Cut a joist having the same dimensions as the original, then bevel one of its edges to ease installation *(inset)*.

◆ With a helper, rotate the new joist into position atop the beam supporting the deck and fasten it to the ledger board and ribbon board with 7-inch galvanized angle plates held by $1\frac{1}{2}$-inch nails.

◆ Nail the two joists together with $3\frac{1}{2}$-inch nails, staggered top and bottom at 12-inch intervals.

◆ Finally, nail the floorboards to the top edge of the new joist.

TRICKS OF THE TRADE

Cure for a Rickety Deck

A simple diagonal brace adds rigidity to a wobbly deck. With a helper, temporarily tack a 1-by-8 board diagonally across the underside of the deck so that when trimmed to fit it can be nailed to the end joists on both sides of the deck. Mark the top of the board along the end joists, then take the board down and cut along the two lines. Nail the board to the underside of each joist with three $2\frac{1}{2}$-inch galvanized nails.

REMOVING PORCH POSTS AND COLUMNS

1. Jacking a porch roof.

◆ Set the jack on a 2-by-12 board and line it up between the roof header and the floor joist nearest the damaged column.

◆ Extend the jack's telescoping tubes so that the top is about 2 inches from the roof header. Lock the tube in place with the steel pins provided.

◆ While a helper holds the jack plumb and steadies a second board atop the jack, extend the jack by turning the screw handle. When the jack is snug against the boards, give the handle a quarter turn—enough for the jack to support the roof without lifting it.

2. Disassembling the support.

◆ To remove a porch post or solid column *(above),* use a handsaw to cut through the post in two places about 1 foot apart. Knock out the middle section with a mallet, and work the top and bottom sections loose. Install a new post using the hardware from the old post.

◆ To remove a hollow column *(above, right),* make two vertical cuts, opposite each other, down the length of the shaft with a circular saw. Then make a horizontal cut around the middle. Pull the two upper sections apart and remove them, staying clear of the capital in case it falls—it may not be nailed to the header.

◆ If the capital is attached to the header, detach it with a pry bar; to free the capital from the post, cut it in two. Remove the two lower shaft sections and the base.

◆ Check the post inside to see if it is damaged, and replace it if necessary. Cover the post with a new shaft, capital, and base.

SALVAGING A DECK SUPPORT

Reusing a ground-level footing.

◆ First, support the deck with a jack set near the damaged post, then cut off the post flush with the top of the footing. Chisel the bottom of the post from the footing.

◆ Fill the resulting cavity with new concrete. Then use a plumb bob to establish the postion of a J bolt, directly under the beam. Push the J bolt into the concrete *(inset).*

◆ When the concrete has cured for 24 to 48 hours, attach a post anchor to the bolt.

◆ Cut a new post to fit between the beam and the post anchor. Nail it to the post anchor and to the beam, using the original hardware if possible.

Building up a buried footing.

◆ To prepare the new footing, support the frame with a jack, dig down to expose the top of the old footing, and cut off the post as close as possible to the footing. Fill the hole with concrete, covering the remnants of the old post by at least 8 inches.

◆ Measure and cut a new post long enough to sink about 1 inch into the new footing, and set it into the concrete.

◆ Hold the post plumb while a helper fastens it at the top. Brace the bottom of the post with scrap lumber to hold it plumb *(inset)*. Allow the concrete to set at least 24 hours before removing the jack.

— NEW CONCRETE
— OLD CONCRETE

Splicing a weak post.

When only the upper or lower part of a porch or deck post is rotten, you can splice in a new section instead of replacing the whole post.

◆ Support the deck on a jack and saw through the post just outside the damaged area. Measure and cut a replacement section long enough to sink into a new footing if one is needed *(above)*.

◆ Cut an L-shaped notch, half the thickness of the post and 6 inches long, in the end of the undamaged section, and a matching notch in one end of the replacement section. Clamp the notched sections together and drill three $\frac{3}{8}$-inch holes through the joint, staggering their positions. Counterbore the holes for nuts and washers, then secure the joint with $\frac{3}{8}$-inch carriage bolts.

◆ Attach the other end of the replacement section to the deck or footing.

Holes, pockmarks, and cracks in concrete can usually be filled with patching mortar. The procedure to use depends on the size of the flaw. Cracks and holes less than 1 inch deep can be brushed clean and filled with tough latex or epoxy patching mortar. Epoxy compounds are slightly stronger and more water-resistant than latex ones.

Major Repairs: Larger flaws must be dressed with a cold chisel before patching. Epoxy and latex mortars may be too expensive for filling big cracks and holes. Moreover, they are unsuitable for mending concrete steps *(opposite bottom)*. Instead, use bonding adhesive and prepackaged patching mortar—a dry mix of sand and cement to which you add water.

A Test for Failed Concrete: Such repairs may not suffice if the concrete around a flaw crumbles when chiseled, a possible sign of wide- spread deterioration. To test for overall soundness, drop a tire iron in several places. A sharp ringing noise indicates firm concrete; a dull thud signals crumbling beneath the surface. Concrete that fails this test is best broken up and rebuilt.

SAFETY TIP

As shown here, wear goggles and gloves when chiseling concrete.

PATCHING A LARGE HOLE OR CRACK

1. Preparing the damaged area.
Chip out the concrete in the damaged area with a cold chisel and a maul to a depth of about $1\frac{1}{2}$ inches. Under- cut the edge slightly so that the bot- tom of the cavity is wider than the top *(inset)*. Clear away the debris, then wet the area with a hose. Blot up ex- cess water with a sponge.

2. Adding the adhesive and mortar.
◆ Brush bonding adhesive evenly around the cavity, and wipe up any spills around the edge of the hole with a rag.
◆ Wait for the adhesive to become tacky—usually from 30 minutes to two hours, depending on the brand— then prepare the sand-and- cement patching mortar ac- cording to the manufac- turer's instructions. Trowel the mixture into the hole be- fore the bonding adhesive can harden.

3. Smoothing the patch.

Level the surface of the mortar by drawing a wood float back and forth across it several times. Remove excess mortar around the edges of the patch with a trowel; then, before the patch hardens, wipe the edge joint smooth with burlap or a rag. Cover the patch with a towel or a piece of burlap. Keep the cloth moist for a week to be sure that the patch cures completely.

REBUILDING A CRUMBLING STEP CORNER

1. Preparing the corner.

◆ Chisel away the damaged corner until you reach solid concrete on all sides, then flatten the bottom of the cavity and undercut the sides slightly. Clear the cavity of debris.

◆ Cut form boards to enclose the corner and contain the mortar. Brace the boards in position, even with the top of the step, and nail their ends together at the corner (right).

◆ Coat the inside of the form boards with motor oil, and paint the cavity with bonding adhesive.

2. Filling in the corner.

◆ After the adhesive has had a chance to become tacky, trowel in sand-and-cement patching mortar and tamp it down to fill the entire hole. As the patch begins to harden, level the surface with a wood float and remove any excess mortar with a trowel.

◆ Cover with burlap and keep the burlap damp for a week.

Rustic Decks and Elegant Porches

The outdoor additions described in this chapter range from a relatively simple-to-build freestanding deck to a wraparound porch with a hip roof anchored to the house. These ambitious structures can challenge an experienced carpenter, yet all are within your reach if you plan ahead, take your time, and proceed in the orderly fashion described on the following pages.

A low, freestanding deck like the 10-foot-square example shown on the following pages combines simplicity and elegance. Supported entirely on posts set well within the perimeter, the structure appears to float above the ground. The basic design applies to any size deck you may want to build and is easily customized with finishing touches that appeal to you (*pages 44-51*). And because this kind of deck requires no connection to the house, you can build it anywhere in your yard.

Design Considerations: Alongside a house, a door onto the deck is a must. If possible, build at an existing door, removing any steps that might hinder construction.

Determine the size and spacing of structural elements for your deck from the charts on page 21. Decking is ordinarily laid over joists spaced 16 inches apart, but diagonal decking calls for 12-inch joist spacing. A railing—mandatory on all decks over 2 feet high and recommended on lower decks—requires the addition of special bridging to keep the posts from twisting the joists they are attached to.

Sketch a plan of your deck that shows all the dimensions. You may need to submit the plan and apply for a building permit; if not, it's wise nonetheless to confirm with local authorities that the design complies with building codes.

At the Lumberyard: Examine each board individually. Avoid curved or twisted planks; they are hard to work with, and the defects can worsen over time, weakening the deck. And while you may prefer redwood or cedar for the decking (*page 26*), choose posts of pressure-treated southern pine rated for ground contact.

Special Materials: Galvanized joist hangers and a variety of other framing connectors greatly simplify deck construction. Galvanized hangers are widely available—as are nails of appropriate diameter and length. Do not substitute common nails, which will make joints that lack the necessary strength. Other fasteners should also be galvanized to prevent rust. Redwood decking, however, requires acid-resistant aluminum nails.

Equipment for the Job: Besides common carpentry tools, you will need a posthole digger and a water level for a day; consider renting them. Your circular saw must be powerful enough to cut heavy, wet pressure-treated wood. Use a carbide-tipped crosscut blade, and back off if the motor slows.

⚠️ **CAUTION** *Before excavating, establish the locations of underground obstacles such as electric, water, and sewer lines, and dry wells, septic tanks, and cesspools.*

 TOOLS

Measuring tape (25-foot)	Hoe
Plumb bob	Trowel
Posthole digger	Water level
Carpenter's level	Circular saw
Mortar tub	Framing square
	Drill with $\frac{1}{2}$-inch bit

 MATERIALS

Mason's cord	2-by-2 pickets
Concrete mix	Common nails
4-by-4 posts	(3-inch and $3\frac{1}{2}$-inch)
2-by-6 or larger framing lumber	Carriage bolts ($\frac{1}{2}$- by 6-inch)
2-by-4 or 2-by-6 decking	Framing connectors and nails
2-by-4 rails	

SAFETY TIPS

Protect your eyes when hammering nails or using a circular saw. Wear a dust mask when cutting pressure-treated lumber, and wash hands thoroughly after handling it.

Diagram labels: TOP RAIL, CAP RAIL, GUARDRAIL, RAILING POST, CLEAT, TREAD, STRINGER, RIBBON BOARD, 4 x 4 POST, CONCRETE FOOTING, BEAM, BRIDGING, END JOIST, JOIST

Anatomy of a deck.

This freestanding deck stands next to the house on 4-by-4 posts embedded in concrete footings reaching below the frostline. The posts support beams of doubled boards secured to the tops of the posts with metal framing con-nectors. Resting on the beams is a frame nailed together with joist hangers as well as other framing connectors and covered with boards nailed to each joist. Bridging pieces brace end joists against twisting by forces exerted by railing posts bolted to the outside of the frame. The railing consists of guardrail, top rail, and cap rail nailed to these posts and filled in with vertical pickets. Easy-to-make steps, consisting of treads on cleats nailed to stringers, lead from the deck to a concrete slab on the ground.

Maximum Joist Span		
JOIST SIZE	**JOIST SPACING**	
	12"	16"
2" x 6"	11' 7"	9' 9"
2" x 8"	15' 0"	12' 10"
2" x 10"	19' 6"	16' 5"

Maximum Beam Span				
BEAM SIZE	**JOIST SPAN**			
	6'	8'	10'	12'
2 x 6s (2)	8'	7'	6'	5'
2 x 8s (2)	10'	9'	8'	7'
2 x 10s (2)	12'	11'	10'	9'
2 x 12s (2)	14'	13'	12'	11'

Spans for joists and beams.

From the chart above choose a joist size for the width of the deck you would like to construct, then use the chart shown at right, above, to select a beam, which is made of two boards nailed together. Joists may extend beyond beams—and beams beyond posts—by $\frac{1}{3}$ the length of the spans in the charts. With this information, you will be able to calculate the number and spacing of posts needed to support the structure.

1. Squaring the layout.

Use triangulation to establish post positions square to the house wall.

◆ Make two marks to indicate the width of the deck on the house. Between these marks make two other marks to indicate post positions.

◆ Hammer a nail partway into the wall at one of the inner marks. Six feet from the nail, drive another. Tie a length of mason's cord to this nail and mark it 10 feet from the nail.

◆ Tie one end of one end of another length of cord to the nail at the post-position mark and the other end to a 1-by-2 stake. Mark this cord 8 feet from the nail.

◆ Pull the cords taut and maneuver them until the marks touch, then drive the stake into the ground. Repeat the process at the other side of the deck. Mark each cord where the outside faces of each post will lie.

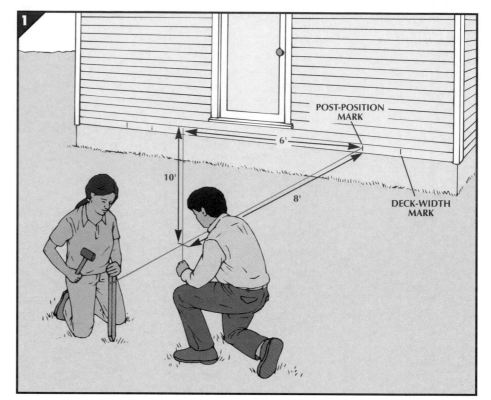

POST-POSITION MARK

6'

10'

8'

DECK-WIDTH MARK

2. Chalking post positions.

◆ Stake 2 cords so they cross the beam marks made in Step 1.

◆ Use a plumb line and chalk mark the ground at the 4 string intersections; remove the strings, leaving the nails and stakes.

◆ With a posthole digger, dig footing holes at the chalk marks. Make each 12 inches across at the top, widening to 16 inches at the bottom. Dig down 24 inches—or 8 inches below the frost-line, whichever is greater.

◆ Pour 8 inches of concrete into the holes and let it set up to 48 hours; retie the strings that you took down to dig the hole.

3. Plumbing the posts.

◆ Set a 4-by-4 post of ample length in one of the holes. Position it at the intersection of the strings as shown at right, taking care not to push the cords out of line. Fasten a 1-by-2 brace to one side of the post with a single nail, then drive a stake into the ground within reach of the brace. While a helper with a level holds the post vertical, nail the brace to the stake. Use the same method to plumb and brace the adjacent side of the post.

◆ After plumbing the other posts, pour concrete into the holes, stopping a few inches below the lip, then replumb the posts as necessary. Allow the concrete to set at least 24 hours before removing the braces. Pack dirt into the hole, sloping the surface to direct runoff away from the post.

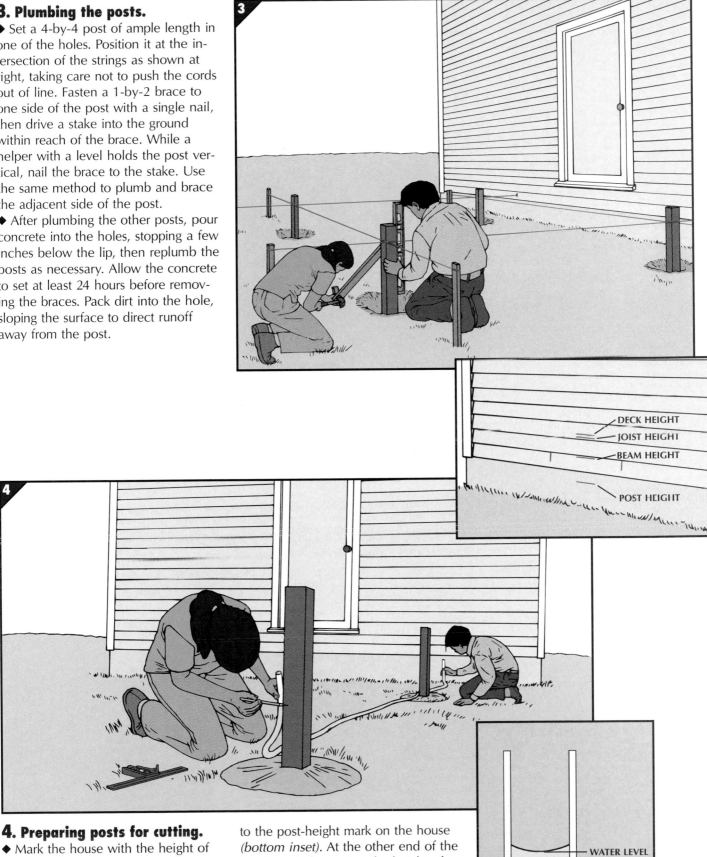

DECK HEIGHT
JOIST HEIGHT
BEAM HEIGHT
POST HEIGHT

WATER LEVEL

4. Preparing posts for cutting.

◆ Mark the house with the height of the deck floor, then measure down a distance equal to the thickness of the decking plus the depth of a joist and a beam *(top inset)*.

◆ Fill a water level. With a helper, adjust the level so that the water comes to the post-height mark on the house *(bottom inset)*. At the other end of the level, mark the post at the height of the water.

◆ Place a combination square at the post-height mark and draw cutting lines on each face of the post. Repeat this process on the remaining posts.

5. Preparing a post for a beam.

Set a circular saw to cut 2 inches deep. Position the lower edge of the blade at the post-height mark and cut across one face of the post. Repeat the process on the other side of the post, then nail a post-and-beam connector *(inset)* to the top of the post.

6. Making and mounting beams.

◆ Cut 4 beam boards the width of the deck, then fasten the boards together in pairs to form beams. Nail the beams with 3-inch galvanized common nails driven in rows of 3 into both sides of the beam at 16-inch intervals. Stagger the nails so that rows on one side fall midway between rows on the other.

◆ Bevel the bottom corners of each beam by cutting along a diagonal line drawn between marks 2 inches from the corner.

◆ Center the beams in the connectors atop the posts, and nail them in place.

A SKELETON OF JOISTS

1. Building the outer frame.

◆ Cut end joists and ribbon boards to length.

◆ To make the frame, drive three $3\frac{1}{2}$-inch nails through the faces of the ribbon boards into the ends of the joists.

◆ With a helper, set the frame on the beams $\frac{1}{2}$ inch from the house wall, end joists even with the ends of the beams.

◆ To square the frame, measure the diagonals *(left)*. If they are not equal, tap the frame with a heavy hammer to make them so.

◆ Use galvanized framing connectors to secure the end joists to the beams *(inset)*, and inside the corners to stiffen the frame.

2. Marking joist locations.

Measuring from the inner face of one end joist, mark one of the ribbon boards at 16-inch intervals, then extend the marks down the face of the board with a framing square. Pencil an X on the side of the line nearest to the starting point. Mark the other ribbon board in the same manner, starting from the same end joist.

◆ Align the inner edge of a joist hanger with each mark, positioning the opening of the hanger over the X and flush with the bottom of the ribbon board (inset). Nail this side of the hanger in place.

◆ Cut all inner joists to length.

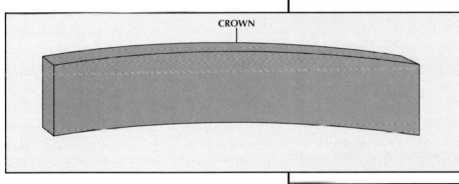

CROWN

A crowned joist.

Most lumber used for deck framing is slightly curved along its length, as shown in the exaggerated depiction at left. Sight down the edge of a board to detect such a curve. Install joists crown up.

3. Installing joists and bridging.

◆ Slide the first inner joist into its joist hangers. Secure each end by holding the hanger closed and nailing it to the ribbon board, then to each side of the new joist.

◆ For a deck that will have a railing, add pieces of bridging to reinforce the end joists after installing the adjacent inner joists. Position the bridging between the joists, offset about 4 inches from each railing-post location (page 21). Drive three $3\frac{1}{2}$-inch common nails through each joist into the ends of the bridging.

◆ Install the remaining inner joists.

PRESSURE-TREATED
PINE

REDWOOD

CEDAR

Types of decking.

You can surface a deck with 2-by-4s, 2-by-6s, or decking stock 1 inch thick with rounded edges *(above, top)*. Pressure-treated pine is the most economical; the greenish tinge often seen in this material bleaches slowly to gray. Alternatives are redwood and cedar, which resist rot naturally. Left untreated, redwood weathers to a dark gray, cedar to a silvery gray. Select decking board by board if possible. Avoid boards that are twisted, crooked, or cupped. If you must use cupped boards, lay them convex side up to shed water.

SPACER

1. Laying the first boards.

◆ Trim a decking board to the width of the deck and lay it about $\frac{1}{8}$ inch from the house wall. Secure it with three 3-inch nails.
◆ Attach subsequent boards, $\frac{1}{8}$ inch apart, with one end flush with one edge of the deck.

2. Laying bowed boards and the final rows.

◆ Position the convex edge of a bowed board against the straight edge of the preceding one. Nail one end to the joist with the usual spacing. Place $\frac{1}{8}$-inch spacers at several joists. Push the board against the spacers and nail the other end in place. Nail the board to the intermediate joists and remove the spacers.
◆ Adjust the spacing of the final 3 feet of decking—or trim one or more boards up to $\frac{1}{4}$ of their width—to bring the last board flush with the edge of the deck.

3. Trimming board ends.

◆ Snap a chalk line across the ends of the boards where they extend beyond the edge of the deck. Use the pretrimmed board at the house to help position the line at the face of the end joist.

◆ Tack a straight board alongside the line as a saw guide, then trim all the decking with a circular saw set to cut slightly deeper than the thickness of the boards.

ALTERNATIVE DECKING PATTERNS

Diagonal decking.

◆ Measuring from an outer corner of the deck frame, mark off equal distances—about half a joist length—on an end joist and the ribbon board.

◆ Nail a decking board at the marks.

◆ Lay subsequent boards on both sides of the first with a $\frac{1}{8}$-inch gap. To span a distance greater than the length of a decking board, cut the ends of two boards to join at the center of a joist.

◆ Within 1 foot of the house—and where boards abut the wall—precut the boards at a 45° angle.

◆ Trim the boards flush with the frame *(Step 3, above).*

TRICKS OF THE TRADE

A Jig for Quick and Easy Angle Cuts

A straight 2-by-2 a couple of feet long and a scrap of plywood with 10 inches of factory edge are the components of a jig for trimming boards at a 45° angle. To make the jig, use a combination square to mark a 45° angle across the middle of the 2-by-2, then screw the plywood to the board with the factory edge along the line *(left)*. Trim away excess plywood.

Hold the jig against a decking board and position the saw with its base against the plywood and its blade aligned with the cutting mark. On the first cut, saw across both the decking and the jig *(dotted line, below)*, using the plywood as a guide. For subsequent cuts, set the end of the jig at the cutting line.

Herringbone decking.

This style of decking is achieved by dividing the deck into two parts and covering each diagonally *(page 27)* in opposite directions.

◆ In a deck that has no joist at the center, install one if you want a symmetrical pattern.

◆ Cover one side of the frame with diagonal decking boards, precutting 45° angles only on those near the house. Nail the decking to all but the center joist.

◆ Cut the overhanging ends flush with deck sides and along the midline of the center joist, then nail the trimmed ends to the center joist.

◆ For the other side of the deck *(above)*, cut a 45° angle on one end of all the decking boards *(both ends of boards near the house)*. At the center joist, butt the boards against the ones that have already been installed, then nail them to the center joist and to all the others.

◆ Mark and cut the overhanging ends flush with the frame.

PICKET RAILINGS FOR SAFETY

1. Cutting a post bevel.

Cut 4-by-4 railing posts to length, then bevel one corner of each.

◆ Determine post length by adding together the height above the deck of the finished railing, the thickness of the decking, and the width of a joist, and then subtracting the thickness of the cap rail. Cut all of the posts to this dimension.

◆ Mark a line across one face of each post, 2 inches from the bottom. Set the base plate of the circular saw to make a 45° bevel and cut along the lines *(right)*.

2. Plumbing and drilling posts.

◆ Draw a line on each post at the point where the top of the decking will meet it. Drive a large finishing nail halfway into each post above the line and just touching it.

◆ Have a helper hold each post in position with its weight resting on the nail while you drill a $\frac{1}{2}$-inch hole through the post and the deck frame. Insert a carriage bolt, fit a washer and nut onto the end, and tighten the assembly so the post moves only when tapped with a hammer.

◆ While the helper plumbs the post with a level, drill another hole and insert a carriage bolt. Tighten both bolts, then remove the finishing nail.

3. Attaching the rails.

◆ Cut 2-by-4 top rails and guardrails; nail them to the inside of the posts, flush with the tops and 2 inches above the deck surface. Secure the butt joints at the corners with 3-inch nails.

◆ Cut 2-by-8 cap rails with 45° angle mitered ends and secure them to the posts and the top rails using $3\frac{1}{2}$-inch nails.

4. Nailing pickets to rails.

Cut 2-by-2 pickets to extend from the underside of the cap rail to the bottom of the lower guardrail, then nail them to both guardrails with $2\frac{1}{2}$-inch nails. Use a piece of 2-by-4 as a spacer to ensure a uniform gap between pickets no more than 4 inches wide.

Stairs to a Low-Lying Deck

Steps for a deck built less than 2 feet above ground level are relatively easy to build, usually requiring no railing or anchors to the ground. Loads imposed on stairs are carried by treads that span descending boards called stringers, usually 2-by-12s. The top of the steps is fastened to the deck; the bottom rests on a concrete slab.

The Math of Stairs: The riddles of steps are how many will be needed and where they will meet the ground. As a first step toward solving them, measure total rise—the distance from the ground to the surface of the deck.

To find the number of steps, divide the total rise by 7 inches—the ideal height of a stair. For the 21-inch-high deck shown on pages 26-29, the number is 3. *(For fractional values, plan for a slightly higher or lower step, add a step, or subtract one)*. Divide the total rise by the number of steps to get unit rise—the actual height of each step.

Allow for steps between 10 and $11\frac{1}{2}$ inches deep, a dimension called the unit run. Multiply this figure by the number of steps to get total run, the horizontal distance between the deck and the front edge of the bottom tread.

If your yard slopes slightly or the slab for the bottom of the steps rises higher than ground level, you may need to refine rise and run figures by repeating the foregoing measurements and calculations.

Meeting the Codes: Stairs are strictly regulated by building codes. Stringers carrying treads made from 2-by-10s, like those shown here, should be separated by no more than 30 inches. Check with local authorities to determine whether you need a stair railing *(pages 46-47)* or anchors for the bottoms of the stringers *(page 65)*.

TOOLS

Folding rule	Circular saw
Carpenter's	Hammer
level	Mortar tub
Framing square	Spade

MATERIALS

2-by-12s	Galvanized
2-by-10s	common nails (3-
2-by-3s	and $3\frac{1}{2}$-inch)
1-by-4s	Concrete mix

1. Establishing rise and run.
◆ Measure the approximate total rise of the steps from the top of the decking to the ground and divide by 7. Multiply the result by the tread depth to get total run. Mark this distance on a carpenter's level with tape.
◆ Rest the level on the deck, aligning the tape with the edge of the decking, then measure actual total rise at the end of the level *(left)*. Chalk a mark on the ground at this point, then measure another 15 inches out from this mark to determine where the front edge of the slab will fall.

2. Preparing the slab.

◆ Dig a hole 6 inches deep for the slab, about 1 foot wider than the stairs and 30 inches from front to back.

◆ Construct a rectangular form of 1-by-4s to fit in the top of the hole, with 1-by-4s nailed to the sides to keep it from falling in. Shim the form to level it.

◆ Fill the hole with concrete and finish it level with the top of the form *(pages 97 and 98)*.

3. Marking unit rise and run.

◆ Recheck rise and run; from a 2-by-12, cut 2 stringers a bit longer than the distance from the top edge of the deck to the slab's front edge.

◆ Position a framing square on one of the boards so that the value for unit run on one arm of the square meets the corner of the board and the value for unit rise on the other arm meets the edge. Draw the unit rise and run on the board as shown above, left, and repeat the procedure for each step. *(Since the deck serves as the top step, only 2 stair treads are necessary.)*

◆ Extend the first unit-run line you drew and the last unit-rise mark across the board *(above, right)*.

◆ Mark the other stringer board as a mirror image of the first.

4. Cutting stringers.

Lay each stringer board across scraps of 4-by-4 or sawhorses. Cut off the ends of the board along the lines extended in the preceding step to produce the trapezoid shape shown in the inset at right.

5. Attaching cleats to stringers.

◆ Draw a line $1\frac{1}{2}$ inches below each unit-run line.

◆ Cut 2-by-3 cleats, mitering the ends for a neat appearance. Position each cleat as shown at right, then secure it with three 3-inch nails.

6. Installing stair treads.

◆ Secure the stringers to the inside faces of the deck railing posts with $3\frac{1}{2}$-inch nails. If you have not built a railing, use framing connectors to attach the stringers to the ribbon board.

◆ Cut 2-by-10 treads to span the distance between the stringers. Position the treads atop the cleats, flush with the front edge of the stringers, and fasten them with 3-inch nails driven into the cleats.

TOP RAIL
HANDRAIL
MIDDLE RAILS
BOTTOM RAIL

2 x 6s
LANDING JOIST
BEAM
RIBBON BOARD
RAMP JOIST
1¼″ DECKING
RIBBON BOARDS
CONCRETE SLAB
GRAVEL
2 x 8

Sloping Access from the Ground

For those who get around with a wheelchair or crutches, a ramp can transform a deck from an obstacle into a delight. Most building codes specify that ramps rise no more than 1 inch for every 12 inches of run (1 in 20 is ideal), so they are practical only for low decks. For example, the 21-inch-high deck shown on the preceding pages would require a slope 21 feet long.

A ramp includes an upper landing at least 36 inches square (42 inches for wheelchairs), a concrete slab at the bottom, and the sloping platform between them. For small decks, a second landing midway in the slope allows a turn for a compact appearance. By augmenting the methods shown beginning on page 22, you can build landings as freestanding additions to any deck.

Landing joists are supported at one end by a beam atop 4-by-4 posts. A ribbon board covers the other ends of the joists and rests on a 2-by-6, one of two attached with ½-inch carriage bolts to opposite sides of a pair of 4-by-4 posts. These posts—and others spaced no more than 5 feet apart along the ramp and joined by 2-by-6s—rest on concrete footings in earth-filled holes and serve as railing posts as well as support for the ramp.

The ramp is framed in modules made of 2-by-6 joists attached to ribbon boards with joist hangers. The top module has an angled end that fits flush against the landing; all other module ends are square. Joints between modules fall at the posts, each module resting on one of the 2-by-6s attached there.

At the bottom of the ramp, joists enter narrow trenches and rest on 2-by-8s laid flat atop undisturbed earth or 2 inches of gravel. The slab rises 1 inch above grade to provide a smooth transition to the 1¼-inch decking.

Railings are nailed to the inner faces of the posts. A 2-by-6, rounded to provide a firm grip, forms a top rail 36 inches above the ramp surface and 2 inches higher than the post tops. The space between the 2-by-4 bottom rail and the ramp surface is no more than 4 inches; middle rails are no more than 6 inches apart. A 1½-inch round handrail is attached at a height convenient for a wheelchair user.

33

A deck that rises 8 or more feet above the ground shares much with similar structures built nearer the ground. For example, joist spans and spacing *(page 21)* are identical to those for a low-lying deck. Decking is also the same.

However, these taller structures require additional rigidity. Some comes from thicker, stiffer posts at the outer edge of the deck, the rest from a piece of lumber called a ledger board. Fastened directly to the house, the ledger board allows the deck to borrow strength from the larger structure.

Design Considerations: The layout of your house is an important factor in planning a high deck. The wall next to the deck must have a door—or a place where a new door can be added. Consider siting the deck with the door close to one end of the deck, to allow you to make the most of your outdoor space.

The overall height of the deck is dictated by the level of the framing for the adjacent house floor, to which the ledger is anchored. The deck surface is positioned 3 inches below the door. Any deck higher than a couple of feet off the ground requires a railing.

Structural Concerns: The technique for attaching the ledger varies according to the type of framing members in the house floor. If your house was built before 1970, it probably has a solid band of lumber for securing the ledger. A newer house, however, may have prefabricated framing components that lack the solid wood needed for anchoring the ledger. In such cases, you will need to strengthen the house framing before building the deck.

If your house has an unfinished basement or a crawlspace, look there to identify the type of framing you have. *(Without such accessibility, check with your local building authorities. They may have the builder's plans on file.)* If the boards resting on the foundation are solid lumber—usually 2-by-10 or 2-by-12—the framing will require no reinforcement.

The opposite is true if you see either I-beams or floor trusses *(page 39)*. I-beams look like their name: A cross section shows top and bottom 2-by-3s or 2-by-4s called flanges joined by a web of plywood or flake board about 10 inches high. Floor trusses are equally recognizable. Between the flanges runs a web of short diagonal pieces that form a zigzag pattern.

Building Codes: All the structural elements of your deck are governed by local building codes. Check them well as you plan your deck— before beginning construction. The design shown here conforms to most codes for decks from 8 feet to 3 stories high. Keep in mind that an inspector will want to check the deck framing and any house reinforcements that you make to accommodate the ledger. Leave your work visible until the inspection is completed.

⚠️ **CAUTION** *Before excavating, establish the locations of underground obstacles such as electric, water, and sewer lines, and dry wells, septic tanks, and cesspools.*

 TOOLS

Plumb bob	Water level
Measuring tape (25-foot)	Circular saw
	Framing square
Posthole digger	Combination square
Carpenter's level	Drill with $\frac{9}{16}$-inch
Chalk line	and $\frac{3}{8}$-inch bits
Ladders	Hand ripsaw

 MATERIALS

Mason's cord
Powdered chalk
Concrete mix
6-by-6s
2-by-8s, 2-by-10s, or 2-by-12s
Lag screws ($\frac{1}{2}$- by $3\frac{1}{2}$-inch)
Carriage bolts ($\frac{1}{2}$- by 6-inch)
Galvanized common nails (3- and $3\frac{1}{2}$-inch)
Framing connectors and nails
Aluminum flashing (7-inch)
Decking

 SAFETY TIPS

Wear goggles when hammering nails or sawing. Use a dust mask when sawing pressure-treated lumber, and wash your hands thoroughly after handling it. When you are sawing or drilling an unfastened board, have a helper steady it.

Components of a second-story deck.
This second-story deck is attached to the side of the house by a ledger board bolted directly to the house framing. Notched 6-by-6 posts embedded in concrete footings that reach below the frostline support a beam of doubled boards, which is bolted to the posts. The deck's joists are fastened to the ledger with joist hangers and to the beam with nails or framing connectors. A ribbon board covers joist ends. The decking and railing are identical to those shown on the freestanding deck *(pages 26-29)*.

LEDGER BOARD

BRIDGING

JOIST

FRAMING CONNECTOR

RIBBON BOARD

BEAM

FOOTING

ERECTING THE POSTS

1. Laying out the deck.
◆ Drop a plumb bob from the center of the door threshold and mark a reference line on the foundation. To do so, hold one arm of a framing square against the foundation with the outer edge of the other arm touching the plumb bob string. Mark the foundation at the corner of the square *(right)*.
◆ With this mark as a reference point, measure in each direction along the foundation to establish the width of the deck. Drive stakes at these points.
◆ Cut 2 pieces of mason's cord at least as long the planned depth of the deck. Tie a string to each stake, then use the squaring technique shown on page 22 to stake the strings at right angles to the house wall.

2. Marking footing positions.

◆ Measuring from the house, mark the beam's outer edge on each string. Stake a third string so that it crosses the first two at these points.

◆ Beginning at a deck-edge string, mark the length of the beam overhang *(page 21),* on the beam string. Drop a plumb bob from that point and spray a chalk mark *(right).* After repeating this process on the other side of the deck, take down the beam string, leaving the stakes in place.

◆ At each chalk mark, dig a hole 16 inches square, extending below the frostline. Pour 8 inches of concrete into each hole. Replace the beam string and allow the concrete to harden up to 48 hours.

BEAM-EDGE MARK

DECK-EDGE STRING

BEAM-EDGE STRING

OUTER STAKE

3. Setting the posts.

◆ Set an uncut post on each footing, with the post corner at the intesection of the deck-edge and beam-edge strings. Pour 4 inches of concrete around the post.

◆ Fasten a 2-by-3 brace, 6 to 8 feet long, to one side of a post with a single nail or screw. Drive a stake into the ground within reach of the brace. While a helper with a 4-foot level holds the post vertical, fasten the brace to the stake. Attach a brace to an adjacent side of the post in the same way, then plumb and brace the other post.

◆ Pack dirt tightly around the posts and allow 24 hours for the concrete to harden.

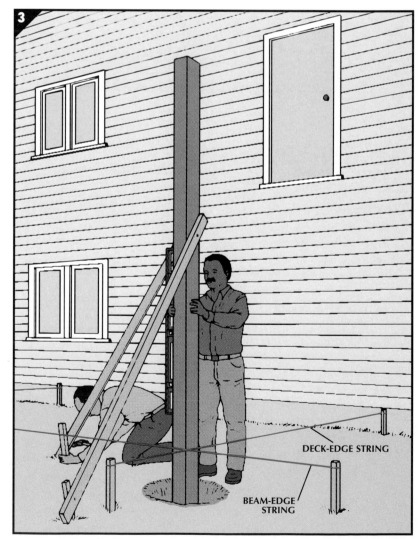

DECK-EDGE STRING

BEAM-EDGE STRING

CUTTING THROUGH SIDING

1. Marking the width on the wall.
Have a helper hold a long, straight board upright against the wall and touching a deck-edge string. While the helper plumbs the board with a 4-foot level, draw a line on the house from a point several inches above the door threshold and extending more than 1 foot below it. Repeat this step at the other side of the deck.

2. Measuring for the cut.
◆ Mark the planned height of the deck surface on the wall below the threshold, then measure down the thickness of the decking to mark the top edge of the ledger. Pencil a similar mark for the bottom of the ledger.
◆ While a helper holds one end of a water level at the ledger top, hold the other end at the vertical line drawn on the wall in Step 1. Mark the line at the height of the water (page 23).
◆ Transfer the height of the ledger bottom by the same means, then repeat the process at the other side of the deck.
◆ Snap chalk lines for the top and bottom of the ledger.

DECK HEIGHT

LEDGER TOP

LEDGER BOTTOM

3. Cutting the siding.
◆ For wood siding, set a circular saw to cut through the siding but no deeper. Begin with a plunge cut *(box, below)* at one end of the area marked for removal. Next, saw along the ledger-top line as far as you can without leaning, then start a similar cut at the ledger-bottom line. Move the ladder and cut along both lines, continuing to the end of the ledger. There, make a vertical cut.
◆ With aluminum siding, follow the same procedure using a metal-cutting blade in the saw. Vinyl siding can be sawed with a blade intended for wood or cut with a utility knife guided by a straightedge.

Beginning a Cut in Siding

TRICKS OF THE TRADE

With your finger off the trigger, retract the blade guard with your thumb. Hold the saw with the back of the blade about 2 inches from the beginning of the cutting line, then rest the front edge of the baseplate on the board and tilt the saw so that the blade is about 1 inch above the line. Grip the saw tightly, switch it on, and pivot the blade slowly into the board. Turn off the saw, and after the blade stops turning, lift it from the cut. Reposition the saw and make another plunge cut to the beginning of the cutting line, and without turning off the saw, push it forward to complete the cut.

Make vertical cuts from the top down. Restart a saw in a cut 1 inch back from your farthest progress. If you hit a nail, back off and start a new plunge cut beyond it. Later, remove wood around the nail with a knife and pull or cut the nail.

---

4. Prying off the siding.
◆ Insert the flat end of a pry bar into the lower cut and lift the siding—wood, aluminum, or vinyl—away from the sheathing. Reach under the siding with wire cutters to sever the exposed nails.
◆ If the nails are too thick to cut, place a wood block under the pry bar to gain enough leverage to pull the siding farther from the wall, freeing the nails.
◆ Discard the siding, and hammer the cut ends of the siding nails flush with the sheathing.

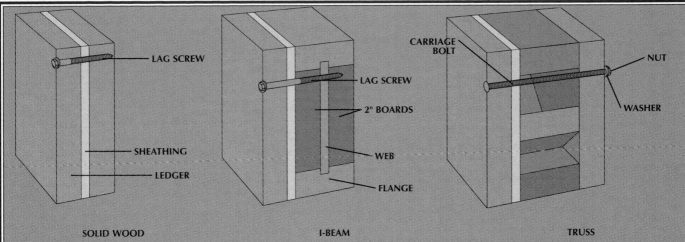

LAG SCREW

SHEATHING

LEDGER

SOLID WOOD

CARRIAGE BOLT

LAG SCREW

2" BOARDS

WEB

FLANGE

I-BEAM

NUT

WASHER

TRUSS

Attachments for Different Framing

In most cases a ledger is fastened with lag screws to the solid wood of a joist or ribbon board in the floor *(above, left)*. Some houses, however, are built with wood I-beams *(above, center)* or trusses *(above, right)*, which require reinforcement. The first step is to expose the inner sides of I-beams and trusses where the ledger will attach to the house. To do so, cut away the ceiling in the room below. Make an opening about 2 feet

wide, measured from the wall, to allow room for hammering.

Reinforcing an I-beam.
Buttress this kind of framing inside and out, the full length of the ledger. Measure the distance between the flanges of the I-beam, and select 2-inch boards to fit. Working through holes in the ceiling, tack them to the plywood web. Outside, cut away sheathing to expose the web. Secure

the boards to the web with carriage bolts, then nail the strip of sheathing back in place. Attach the ledger with lag screws.

Reinforcing a truss.
Strengthen a section at least as long as the ledger with 2-by-10s or 2-by-12s, whichever match the truss height. Attach the boards to the truss with 3-inch nails. Fasten the ledger to this board with carriage bolts.

5. Installing flashing.

◆ Cut strips of 7-inch-wide flashing to span the ledger opening, allowing for a 3-inch overlap between sections. Make a strip approximately 12 inches long for each end of the ledger.

◆ Bend each strip lengthwise, 4 inches from the edge. Push the 4-inch leg of the flashing under the siding, cutting slots for siding nails you encounter. Cut the end pieces so they can be folded to enclose the top corners of the ledger *(inset)*. Friction will hold the flashing in place until the ledger is installed.

HANGING A LEDGER BOARD

1. Marking joist locations.

◆ Cut 4 straight pieces of joist lumber to deck width, one for the ledger, one for the ribbon board, and two for the beam. Clamp the pieces together, edges and ends aligned.

◆ With a combination square, mark the edges of the boards at 16-inch intervals, then pencil an X beside each line, away from the starting point.

◆ Unclamp the boards and extend the lines down the face of the one to be used as the ledger board. Install joist hangers as described on page 25, and attach an all-purpose hanger $1\frac{1}{2}$ inches from each end of the ledger.

◆ Starting 6 inches from one end, drill $\frac{9}{16}$-inch holes at 2-foot intervals, staggered as shown here *(inset)*.

2. Attaching the ledger.

◆ With a helper, lift the ledger into position under the flashing. Drive 3-inch nails at 2-foot intervals to hold the ledger in place.

◆ Fold the flashing over the face and corners of the ledger. To secure the flashing, nail it to the face and ends of the ledger with common nails.

◆ For mounting the ledger to a joist or reinforced I-beam in a house, bore $\frac{3}{8}$-inch holes for $\frac{1}{2}$- by $3\frac{1}{2}$-inch lag screws, using the holes already drilled in the ledger as guides. With trusses, bore $\frac{9}{16}$-inch holes for carriage bolts.

NOTCHING POSTS AND CONSTRUCTING A FRAME

1. Marking and cutting posts to height.
◆ With a water level, mark each post at the height of the top of the ledger board. Extend the mark around all four sides of each post.
◆ Trim the posts to height, beginning with a circular saw and finishing the job with a hand saw.

2. Marking post tops.
With a square, mark the top of each post for a beam notch as shown at left, taking care that the notch faces away from the house (below). The width of the notch is always 3 inches, and the depth is equal to the width of the ledger board and beam lumber.

3. Cutting the notches.

◆ With a circular saw set to its maximum depth, cut across the top of the post and the side facing away from the house along the lines drawn in Step 2.

◆ Finish cutting out the notch with a handsaw. A ripsaw with about 8 teeth per inch is the most efficient tool for the vertical cut; nearly any saw will do for the small amount of wood remaining in the horizontal cut.

4. Attaching the beam.

◆ Make a beam *(page 24, Step 6)* with the boards' marked edges at the top. Set it in the notches of the posts, with equal overhangs. Toenail a 3-inch nail through the bottom of the beam into each post.

◆ On a diagonal across the notch—and at least 2 inches from the top or sides of the post—drill two $\frac{1}{2}$-inch holes through the beam and post. Secure the beam with $\frac{1}{2}$- by 6-inch carriage bolts.

◆ If the deck has more than 2 posts, drill and bolt the beam to interior posts after tightening the bolts at the ends.

5. Attaching the joists.

◆ Nail a multipurpose framing anchor to one end of a joist. Rest the board on the beam and nail the anchor to the ledger *(right)*.

◆ To install interior joists, place one end on the beam and the other in a joist hanger. Hold the hanger closed, then nail it first to the ledger, then to the joist.

◆ Use the marks atop the beam to align the joists perpendicular to the ledger. Secure each joist to the beam with a right-angle framing connector or with 3-inch nails toenailed through the joist into the beam, two on one side and one on the other.

6. Trimming the joists.

◆ Mark the joist length atop the two end joists, then snap a chalk line between these points across the tops of the interior joists. Use a square to extend the chalk marks down one side of each joist.

◆ Lay a 4- by 8-foot sheet of $\frac{1}{2}$-inch plywood on the joists as a work platform. Kneeling on the plywood, trim the joist ends with a circular saw, always cutting on the same side of the lines to ensure equal joist lengths.

7. Nailing the ribbon board.

◆ With the ribbon board on the ground, hammer three $3\frac{1}{2}$-inch nails into the board as follows: Below each mark made on page 40, Step 1, place one nail 1 inch from the top, one 1 inch from the bottom, and the third midway between the first two. The nail tips should barely protrude from the other side.

◆ With a helper to support one end of the ribbon board, nail it to the other end joist. While the helper raises or lowers the ribbon board to align it, nail it to the next joist and then to the remaining joists in succession.

Modifications to the structure of a deck allow you to adapt it to your own tastes. A stairway provides access to the yard from a second-story deck. An angled railing adds a touch of elegance, and benches provide built-in convenience. Joists cut to different lengths allow variations in deck shape. You can even frame a hole to accommodate a favorite shade tree.

Any option you add must conform to building codes, which govern everything from the spacing of stair rails to the method of attaching a bench. Submit plans to local authorities early to avoid last-minute changes at inspection time.

Variations in Technique: Any of these options may call for unusual construction methods. A hole or a cutaway corner, for example, requires adjustments to the framing before the deck is surfaced. The

angled railing, on the other hand, is installed in holes cut through the decking. And stairs, whose stringers may be no more than 30 inches apart, should precede deck railings because railing posts at the top of the stairs can help support the deck railing as well.

Building a Landing: Most codes require a landing for stairs higher than 8 feet. Base the height of the landing on a multiple of the unit rise *(page 30)*. A landing must be at least 36 inches square. The distance between landing and deck is determined by the number of risers above the landing multiplied by the unit run—typically about 10 inches. Subtracting 15 inches from the result lets the upper section of the stairs rest on the landing. If the calculations produce an awkward position for the landing, you may want to modify the deck plans.

TOOLS

Deck-building tools
(pages 20, 30, and 34)
Carpenter's
protractor
T bevel

MATERIALS

Galvanized common nails ($3\frac{1}{4}$-inch)	Joist hangers, single and double
Galvanized finishing nails (2-, 3-, and $3\frac{1}{4}$-inch)	Concrete Mason's cord 1-by-2s
Masonry nails (3-inch)	2-by-6, 2-by-10, and 2-by-12 framing stock
Carriage bolts ($\frac{1}{2}$-inch)	4-by-4 and 6-by-6 posts

VARIATIONS ON THE RECTANGLE

1. Altering the frame.

To shape the corners or edges of a deck, construct the framing as shown on pages 22-25 or 35-43, then cut away portions for the profile you want.

◆ For an angled corner, mark the end joist for cutting between the outside corner and the supporting beam, then make a mark on the ribbon board at the same distance from the corner. Cut both boards at the marks you have just made, removing the corner of the frame.

◆ Measure the distance between the outside edges of the cut frame members *(inset)*, and transfer this measurement to a length of ribbon-board stock.

2. Closing the cutaway corner.

◆ To make a corner board, cut along the marks with a circular saw set at a 45° angle. Bevel the board so the outer face is longer than the inner one.
◆ Drill pilot holes in the ends of the corner board, then secure it to the end joist and ribbon board with $3\frac{1}{2}$-inch nails.

By cutting the frame elsewhere along the deck edge, you can create different shapes. Shortening a joist near the midpoint of an edge and adding angled ribbon boards creates a notch. Cutting the joists progressively longer from two corners of the deck out to the midpoint of one edge creates a curve *(inset)*.

3. Fitting an angled railing.

◆ After installing decking, add at least two 4-by-4 railing posts to each railing segment *(pages 28-29)*.
◆ Cut top rails slightly long and support a side top rail on nails driven partway into the posts. Hold the corner top-rail under the side rail, and mark the intersection points on both faces of each board.
◆ Take down the rails and connect the points with a line across the edge, then bevel both rails with a circular saw.

SIDE TOP RAIL

CORNER TOP RAIL

ADDING A STAIRWAY

1. Locating the bottom of the stairs.

◆ From a scrap of 2-by-12 lumber, cut a pitch block—a right-angle triangle with a 50° angle at one corner.
◆ Tack the pitch block to the deck where you plan to install a stair carriage *(inset)*. Stretch a string along the edge of the pitch block, and chalk a mark where the string meets the ground. Do the same for the other carriage.
◆ Enclose the chalk marks in a rectangle 6 inches wider and longer than a stair tread, with the front of the rectangle 2 inches in front of the marks *(dotted line)*. Dig a 6-inch-deep hole, pour and finish a slab *(page 31),* and wait 24 hours before proceeding.

2. Installing the stairs.

◆ Cut 2-by-10 carriages *(page 64)*, making the first tread below the stair top 1½ inches deeper than the others. Cut 2 facing boards, using a carriage as a template for cutting the ends.

◆ Nail the facing boards to the carriages, then nail each assembly to the deck, tops against the underside of the decking *(right)*.

◆ Nail the carriages to a 2-by-6 fitted between them on the slab, then drive four 3-inch masonry nails through the 2-by-6 into the slab. Add stair treads to the carriages *(page 32)*.

FACING BOARD

3. Adding stair-railing posts.

◆ At intervals less than 5 feet, bolt 4-by-4 railing posts to the carriages *(page 29)*. Set posts with the bottom edge nearest the deck aligned with the bottom carriage edge. *(At the top of the stairs, the stair railing shares posts with the deck railing.)*

◆ Use a framing square to mark the carriage-post tops for cutting; rest the tongue *(short arm)* on the edge of the facing board and pencil a line along the end of the body *(right)*.

4. Attaching the rails.

◆ Tack a 2-by-6 top rail to the posts, edge flush with the post tops. Draw lines across the rail at the outer edges of the top and bottom posts.

◆ Remove the board, cut it along the lines, and attach it with three 3-inch nails into each post.

◆ Mark and cut lower rails in the same manner, allowing gaps of no more than 4 inches between them.

5. Attaching the handrail.

◆ On the top rail, rest a 2-by-6 handrail long enough to extend about 4 inches beyond the bottom stair post.

◆ Mark the edge of the board on both sides of the top post and draw lines at these marks across the face of the handrail board. Between these lines draw another line $3\frac{1}{2}$ inches from the railing edge and parallel to it.

◆ Use these marks as guides for a 2-sided notch in the end of the handrail *(inset)*, cut so that the end and the outside edge of the handrail fit flush with the top post.

◆ Mark and notch the other handrail in the same way, then nail the handrails to the posts and top rails.

BUILDING TO FIT THE SPACE

A stairway landing.

A landing is a miniature deck with doubled ribbon boards in lieu of a beam, joists spaced at 16-inch intervals, and standard decking. The ledger is anchored to wall studs with lag screws, and notched 6-by-6 posts support the ribbon board. For a freestanding landing, a second pair of posts can substitute for a ledger board, as long as postholes are dug more than 8 inches from the house foundation. The height of a landing is a whole-number multiple of the height of a step.

An aperture in a deck.
◆ To frame an opening—around a tree, for example—begin by doubling the joists on both sides of the hole. Double-wide joist hangers are available for this purpose.

◆ Between the doubled joists, insert headers, also made of two thicknesses of joist stock.

◆ For every joist location spanned by the headers, place a partial joist between the header and the ledger board on one side of the opening and, on the other side, between the header and the ribbon board.

◆ After the decking is in place, erect a railing around the opening.

DOUBLED JOIST

HEADER

PARTIAL JOIST

SLANTED RAILINGS FOR A DECK

1. Cutting postholes.
◆ On the decking, mark openings $3\frac{3}{4}$ inches wide and $3\frac{7}{8}$ inches long, with the shorter dimension $1\frac{1}{4}$ inch from the deck edge. Position openings within 16 inches of the corners and no more than 5 feet apart. Along the ribbon board, each opening must have one long side adjacent to a joist.

◆ Drill 15° angled holes at the corners of each rectangle, tilting the top of the drill toward the edge of the deck. Saw the long sides with a saber saw set for a vertical cut; on the short sides, set the saw for a 15° cut.

◆ Nail bridging *(page 25)* next to one edge of each opening along the end joists.

2. Attaching the posts.

Follow the procedure on page 29 to install a 4-by-4 post in each corner hole, bolting each one to a joist or bridging. However, instead of anchoring the posts in a vertical position, use a carpenter's protractor to slant them at an angle of 15° *(left)*. Under the deck, align the inner corner of the post with the bottom of the adjacent joist or bridging.

◆ Measure 36 inches up from the deck surface on the inner face of each post. Stretch a string between the marks and use it to align the inner faces of the remaining posts as you install them.

◆ Make a cutting mark across each post at the height of the string, then set a circular saw for a 15° cut and trim the post tops level.

3. Adding the rails.

◆ Drive a nail partway into each post $5\frac{1}{2}$ inches from the top to support a 2-by-6 rail.

◆ Butt a rail board against the house, its end extending beyond the deck corner. Set the adjoining rail against the first. Mark the first board where the second touches its lower edge *(left)*. Mark the bottom edge of the second board 3 inches from the end.

◆ With a protractor set at $14\frac{1}{2}$°, extend cutting lines from the marks across the faces of the rails, making the top edges longer than the bottom ones.

◆ Miter the boards along these lines with a circular saw set at 44°, cutting so that the outer face of the board is the longer.

◆ Nail the rails to the posts and to each other, then add more rails, spaced no more than 4 inches apart, in the same manner *(inset)*.

VERTICAL SUPPORT

TRIM

Elements of a built-in bench.

This wraparound bench uses an angled railing *(pages 48-49)* for a backrest. The lower rails on each side of the stair opening are cut away to accommodate vertical supports cut from 2-by-12s to match the angles of the railing posts and trimmed in 1-by-2 lumber at the base. Seat planks made of 2-by-6s rest on the supports, which are set at 30-inch intervals and nailed to the railings and decking.

1. Making bench supports.

◆ Cut 17-inch-long pieces of 2-by-12, one for each support required.
◆ Set the handle of a T bevel on the decking and align the blade with the bottom rail. Draw a line at this angle passing through a corner and across the face of a 2-by-12 support blank. Clamp the blank to a work surface and cut along the line.
◆ Use this support as a template for the others. Make one of them the same shape as the first; cut the others $1\frac{1}{2}$ inches narrower to account for railing thickness *(inset)*.

$1\frac{1}{2}$"

2. Installing the supports.

◆ With a circular saw, trim $1\frac{1}{2}$ inches from the 2 bottom rails at the stair opening. Position an end support against the post and the rail ends, and drive two $3\frac{1}{4}$-inch nails through the support into the end of each rail. Toenail the support to the decking with 3 nails angled through each side.

◆ Install intermediate supports at intervals of 30 inches or less. If a support falls at a post, move it far enough to one side to allow nailing through railings. Toenail support bottoms to the decking *(inset)*.

◆ Hide the toenails with strips of 1-by-2 lumber fastened to the supports with 2-inch finishing nails.

3. Attaching seat planks.

◆ Miter one end of four 2-by-6s at a 45° angle to fit together at a corner. Tack the planks to the supports leaving $\frac{1}{8}$ inch between the boards. Over the midpoint of each support, pencil a mark on the unmitered end, staggering the marks to fall at different supports.

◆ Remove the planks, cut them, and nail them in place with three $3\frac{1}{4}$-inch nails at each support.

◆ Plank the other corners in the same way, then measure, cut, and install intermediate planks.

◆ To make a herringbone corner *(inset)*, leave the plank ends square and butt them end to edge.

A porch can improve the appearance and increase the value of your home. The wraparound design shown on the following pages goes best with a large house, but you can easily modify the design to build a porch along one side of your house.

Either structure is a major undertaking. Before you break ground to begin construction, contact your local building authority for a building permit and the required schedule of site inspections.

Planning a Porch: Regardless of the shape you intend for your porch, draw a detailed sketch of the structure, making sure that it satisfies local codes. Position piers so that the concrete footings beneath them will not encounter underground utilities. Ideally, piers and the roof supports above them should frame rather than block doors and windows. If your property slopes more than 3 feet in 8, have a professional excavator level it. Concrete steps or sidewalks may need to be partially demolished.

In most porches, the floor lies one step—6 to $7\frac{1}{2}$ inches—below the threshold of the door into the house. For a wraparound porch, plan wings of equal depth no greater than 10 feet. Doing so will enable you to build a roof with the relatively simple techniques shown on pages 66-77.

Lumber for the Frame: A porch 10 feet deep is supported on joists and beams of 2-by-8s. For narrower structures, consult the chart on page 21. Pressure-treated southern pine is the wood of choice. For every running foot of porch, you'll need 12 to 15 feet of 2-by-8.

Estimating Materials for Piers: Use the depth of your footing *(page 56)* in the formula on page 88 to calculate how much concrete to buy. Dry concrete mix is available in bags or you can buy it from a ready-mix company *(page 96)*.

Build the piers with standard construction-grade cored bricks. Pier height is the finished height of the porch floor, less the thickness of a floor board, the height of a joist, and a small amount to slope the porch for drainage *(page 88)*.

After calculating pier height, use a mason's rule—marked in inches on one side and in courses (rows) of brick on the other—to determine how many courses of brick each pier will require. Add one course to compensate for starting the pier below grade. Multiply the number of rows by the number of bricks in each *(page 57)* and again by the number of piers, then add 5 percent for waste.

Lay the bricks with mortar mix formulated for outdoor use. One cubic foot of mortar will bond 25 to 30 bricks.

Beyond the Basic Structure: Once the floor and stairs are in place, you can add a roof *(pages 66-75)* and a ceiling *(page 76)*, as well as a railing and columns *(page 77)*. When the porch is completed, paint the floor and the stairs with a finish coat made especially for porches and decks.

 Before excavating, establish the locations of underground obstacles such as electric, water, and sewer lines, and dry wells, septic tanks, and cesspools.

 TOOLS

Hammer drill	Spade
Circular saw	Posthole digger
Hammer	Mason's trowel
Mason's level	Convex jointer
Plumb bob	Mason's rule
Try square	Utility knife
Framing square	Caulk gun
Water level	Power floor nailer
Power screwdriver	and mallet

M MATERIALS

Concrete	Silicone caulk
Bricks	Wood preservative
Mortar	Wood putty
Powdered chalk	Joist hangers
2-by-4s	Joist-hanger nails
1-by-6s	Framing anchors
2-inch framing lumber	Lag screws ($\frac{1}{2}$- by 4-inch)
1-inch fascia board	Lag shields ($\frac{1}{2}$-inch)
Tongue-and-groove flooring	Masonry drill bit ($\frac{3}{4}$-inch)
Aluminum flashing	Drill bit ($\frac{9}{16}$-inch)

 SAFETY TIPS

Wear goggles or other eye protection when hammering or using a power saw, a dust mask when cutting pressure-treated lumber, and gloves when working with wet mortar.

FASCIA **LEDGER BOARD** **JOISTS** **CARRIAGE** **FLASHING** **JACK JOIST** **LATTICE** **DOUBLED CORNER JOIST** **BAND BEAM** **BRICK PIER** **CONCRETE FOOTING**

Anatomy of a wraparound porch.

Brick piers built on concrete footings support a doubled band beam at the perimeter of the 8-foot-wide porch shown above. The larger central corner pier bears the additional load carried by a doubled corner joist. A ledger board bolted to the house wall sup- ports the inner edge of the porch. Flashing prevents water from seeping behind the ledger board. Joists of 2-by-8 lumber between the ledger and the band beam—and shorter jack joists between the band beam and the cor- ner joist—underlie a floor made of $\frac{3}{4}$- by $3\frac{1}{4}$-inch tongue-and-groove boards. The carriages that support a wide set of steps are fastened at the top to the band beam and rest at the bottom on a shallow concrete footing. A fascia board covers the rough lumber of the band beam, and lattice skirts enclose the crawl space underneath the porch.

CONSTRUCTING A LEDGER BOARD

1. Marking hole positions.

◆ Cut away house siding with a circular saw $\frac{1}{4}$ inch above the planned height of the porch floor *(page 38)*.
◆ From the straightest lengths of joist lumber available, cut ledger-board pieces for each porch wing. Make one ledger board $1\frac{1}{2}$ inches longer than the length of the wing it will support.
◆ Four inches from one end of each ledger board—and every 16 inches thereafter—make a pencil mark on the centerline.
◆ Alternating 2 inches above and below the centerline, drill a $\frac{9}{16}$-inch bolt hole opposite each mark.

LEDGER BOARD

4" 16"

2. Installing the ledger board.

◆ Nail the board to the house wall—level, and $\frac{3}{4}$ inch below the porch-floor height.

◆ For a concrete foundation, bore $2\frac{1}{2}$ inches into the concrete through the lower holes with a hammer drill and a $\frac{3}{4}$-inch masonry bit, then seat expansion shields in the holes with the bit. Other foundation materials require a different approach *(box, below)*.

◆ Fasten the ledger to the concrete with $\frac{1}{2}$- by 4-inch lag screws and washers.

◆ Secure the upper half of the ledger board according to your house framing *(page 39)*.

HAMMER DRILL

FOUNDATION

Dealing with Other Types of Masonry

LEDGER BOARD

BACKING BOARD

CARRIAGE BOLT

CONCRETE BLOCK

To attach a ledger board to brick, hollow block, or a veneered surface, bolt it through a backing board on the other side of the foundation. Doing so requires access to the ledger location from inside the foundation—simple enough in an unfinished basement or tall crawlspace, more challenging in a finished basement.

Proceed by nailing the ledger in place and using ledger bolt holes *(page 53)* as guides to bore $\frac{3}{4}$-inch holes through the foundation with a hammer drill. Tack a 2-by-4 or wider backing board over the row of holes in the house interior, and use the foundation holes as guides to drill through the backing board. Place a $\frac{1}{2}$- by 12-inch carriage bolt in each hole. Inside the foundation, put a washer and nut on each bolt, and tighten securely.

PLANNING AND POURING FOOTINGS

PERIMETER MARKER

BATTER-BOARD STAKE

1. Stakes for batter boards.

◆ Lay out a pattern of 5 small stakes as rough perimeter, or boundary, markers. Place stakes at the 3 corners of the porch and at the 2 points where the house walls, if extended, would intersect the perimeter *(dotted lines)*.

◆ Cut sixteen 2-by-4 stakes about 1 foot longer than porch height for batter boards. Drive pairs of stakes about 2 feet outside the perimeter markers, then remove the markers.

2. Erecting batter boards.

◆ With a water level *(page 23)*, mark the height of the top of the ledger board on the 2-by-4 stakes.

◆ Measure down from this mark a distance equal to the width of the ledger board ($7\frac{1}{2}$ inches for a 2-by-8) plus an amount for drainage—$\frac{1}{8}$ inch for each foot that the porch extends from the house. A mark at this point establishes pier height.

◆ Screw a 1-by-6 batter board to each pair of stakes with the top at pier height, making sure that the board is level.

3. Stringing boundary lines.

◆ Hammer nails partway into the bottom of the ledger, one nail 8 inches from each end and one at the central corner.

◆ Tie 2 lengths of mason's cord to the corner nail, then use the squaring method described on page 22, Step 1 to align each string perpendicular to a house wall. Where each string crosses a batter board, hammer a small nail and loop the string around it.

◆ To establish the perimeter of the porch *(left)*, adapt the method for squaring a layout shown on page 36. Measure the diagonals of the two rectangles and one square formed by the strings as on page 24, Step 7 to make sure the layout is square.

4. Establishing footing locations.

◆ For footings between corners, mark evenly spaced pier centers on the boundary and end lines of each wing. Space them no farther apart than the maximum span allowed for doubled beams of your joist lumber—9 feet for 2-by-8s *(page 21)*. Drop a plumb line 8 inches to either side of each mark and chalk an X as shown at left, then outline a 12- by 16-inch rectangle at each pier position.

◆ For the pier at the end of each wing, drop a plumb bob from the intersection of the boundary and end strings to establish the center of the pier. Chalk an X at that point, then outline a 12- by 16-inch rectangle on the ground, straddling the end line.

◆ Repeat the process at the boundary-line intersection to mark the corner of the pier at the central corner, but chalk a 16- by 16-inch square on the ground.

PIER PERIMETER

5. Constructing the footings.

◆ Unhook one end of each batter-board string.

◆ With a spade and a posthole digger, excavate footing holes at least 4 inches larger in each dimension than the outlines chalked on the ground. Dig 24 inches deep or 8 inches below the frostline, whichever is greater, then tamp the soil at the bottom to compact it.

◆ Pour concrete into each hole to a height 3 inches below ground level. Slice through the wet concrete with a spade in order to remove air bubbles and push large pebbles below the surface.

◆ Cover the footings with moist burlap and allow them to set for 24 to 48 hours.

6. Marking footings for piers.

◆ Reattach the boundary lines to the batter boards.

◆ Outline the shapes of the piers on the footings as you did on the ground in Step 4 above, using a try square to make accurate corners. Take down the boundary strings.

BUILDING BRICK PIERS

1. Laying the bricks.

◆ With a mason's trowel, spread a $\frac{3}{8}$-inch layer of mortar inside the pier outline. Furrow the mortar with the point of the trowel. Lay the first course of well-dampened bricks, buttering adjoining surfaces with $\frac{3}{8}$ inch of mortar. *(For a 16- by 16-inch pier, duplicate the pattern that is shown in the top inset at right.)*

◆ Trowel away excess mortar, then level and square the first course before laying the next.

◆ Stagger the joints in succeeding courses as shown in the bottom inset at right. At the end of each course, shape and smooth the joints with a convex jointer.

2. Completing the piers.

◆ When you have laid bricks to a point 4 or 5 courses below the planned height of the pier, gauge your progress with a mason's rule and a level set atop a batter board—or re-attach the boundary line as a guide. If the distance to build is not an even multiple of the average height per course of the bricks you've already laid, adjust the thickness of the mortar joints on the remaining courses to compensate.

◆ After you have built all the piers, remove the batter boards and stakes.

MASON'S RULE

3. Installing J-bolt anchors.
◆ Fill the piers to a point 8 inches below the top with rubble such as stones and chipped brick, then with mortar to the top.
◆ Before the mortar dries, insert a $\frac{1}{2}$- by 8-inch J bolt in each pier. For the large corner pier *(left),* position the J bolt so it will not obstruct the porch's corner joist. Elsewhere, plant the bolt in the center of the pier. In every case, allow $2\frac{1}{2}$ inches of bolt threads to protrude from the mortar.

J BOLT

WEATHERPROOFING THE LEDGER

1. Flashing the top and ends.
◆ Loosen or remove house siding above the ledger to allow for flashing installation.
◆ Follow the instructions on page 39 to install flashing at both ends of the ledger and along the top of both wings to within 3 inches of the house corner.
◆ Cut 2 pieces of flashing to make a cap for the ledger corner: Make one piece $7\frac{1}{2}$ inches by 6 inches, and the other $7\frac{1}{2}$ inches by 10 inches.

2. Fabricating corner pieces.

◆ Measure and mark the smaller piece of flashing as shown above, top. Cut along the solid lines with a utility knife, then using the edge of a table or a level, bend the flashing along the dotted lines to form the shape shown above, bottom.

◆ Follow the same procedure to mark, cut, and fold the larger piece of flashing into the shape in the illustration above right.

◆ The illustration at right shows how the 2 pieces overlap to protect the ledger corner.

3. Installing corner flashing

◆ Slip the upper edge of the smaller piece under the house siding at the ledger corner. Nail the flashing to the face of the ledger.

◆ Lay a bead of caulk where the seam between the two corner pieces will lie.

◆ Install the larger corner flashing piece. Fit it snugly over the smaller piece of flashing and the corner of the ledger. Nail it to the ledger face.

◆ Caulk all flashing seams.

ASSEMBLING THE SUBSTRUCTURE

JOIST LOCATIONS

1. Establishing joist positions.

Align the body of a framing square with the top edge of the ledger at the end of one wing. Mark the sides of joist positions every 16 inches from the end of the ledger. To allow room for the installation of the doubled corner joist, adjust the position of the last full-length joist, if necessary, so it is no closer than 5 inches to the ledger corner.

CUT MARK

2. Installing the first joists.

◆ On the top and the side of each pier, scribe a line 3 inches from the outer face of the pier and parallel to the house to mark the thickness of the double band beam.
◆ Select a piece of lumber for an end joist, crown it *(page 25)*, and position it as shown at left. Make a cut mark where the board crosses the line scribed on the pier.
◆ Cut the joist to length. Attach a multipurpose framing anchor to the end with joist-hanger nails, then nail the hanger to the ledger. Repeat the procedure for the joist at the end of the other wing.
◆ Install a joist at each of the remaining 12- by 16-inch piers, attaching them to the ledger with joist hangers. Pier joists may pass no closer than 2 inches from J bolts; shift the joists slightly along the ledger as needed to satisfy this requirement.

INNER BAND BEAM

3. Starting the inner band beam.

◆ Cut a piece of joist lumber to extend from an end joist to a point 3 inches beyond the joist resting on the adjacent pier, then nail it to the ends of both joists with three $3\frac{1}{2}$-inch nails *(left)*.
◆ Trim another beam section to reach 3 inches past the next joist and nail it in place. Work along both wings of the porch toward the corner pier. Where the band beams meet, nail through the face of one into the end of the other. *(Loose joints between band-beam sections will be secured in the next step when the band beam is doubled.)*
◆ Measure and cut joists to fit between the ledger board and the band beam *(above right)*. Attach one end of each joist to the ledger with a joist hanger and nail the band beam to the other end.

END
JOIST

STRING

TRICKS OF THE TRADE

Compensating for an Uneven House Wall

A band beam will mimic undulations in a house wall unless you cut joists to compensate. To find the length for each joist, tie a string above the ledger to nails tapped into the narrow space between the ledger and the joists resting on the first and last small pier of each wing. Sight past the string to a tape measure at each joist location. Note how far the ledger bows in or out and add the distance to—or subtract it from—the length of either end joist, then cut a joist to that measure.

BLOCKING

BLOCKING

4. Securing the frame.

◆ To anchor the porch, select a scrap of joist lumber to serve as blocking. At the small piers *(above, left)*, set the piece on top of the J bolt and against the band beam. Tap the blocking with a hammer and drill a $\frac{3}{4}$-inch hole at the resulting mark. Fasten the board to the bolt with a nut and a washer, then drive 3 nails through the band beam into the blocking.

◆ At the corner pier *(above, right)*, fit blocking against one arm of the band beam, trimming as necessary to fit the blocking between the beam and the space to be occupied by the corner joist. Bolt the blocking in place, then nail the beam to it.

Finish the band beam by installing a second, outer set of boards alongside those that are already nailed to the blocking. Cut the outer boards to offset the joints between them from the joints between the inner set. Nail the inner and outer beam boards to each other every 8 inches from alternate sides with three $2\frac{1}{2}$-inch nails. Drive additional nails on both sides of every joint.

5. Making a doubled corner joist.

◆ Measure the distance between the ledger corner and inside corner of the band beam. Mark this distance, plus $1\frac{1}{2}$ inches, on 2 pieces of joist lumber.

◆ Lay the boards edge to edge, crowns outward. Without turning the boards over, cut parallel 45° miters at the ends of each board, then set the boards face to face so that the miters form a point at one end and a V at the other. Nail the boards together from both sides at 16-inch intervals, staggering the rows of nails *(right)*.

◆ Nail a multipurpose framing anchor to each side of the joist at the V-shaped end *(inset)*.

◆ Install the joist, bending the hangers to fit the ledger. Use joist-hanger nails at the ledger, and drive 4-inch nails through the band beam into the pointed end of the joist.

FRAMING ANCHOR

6. Installing jack joists.

◆ Starting at the corner, mark jack-joist positions, 16 inches apart, on the band beams.

◆ Measure from each mark to the corner joist and cut jack joists with one end mitered to a 45° angle.

◆ Tap a U-shaped joist hanger onto the outer end of each jack joist. While a helper holds the joist in place, nail the mitered end to the corner joist. Then nail the joist hanger to the beam and the joist.

◆ Install the rest of the jack joists, alternating sides as you work.

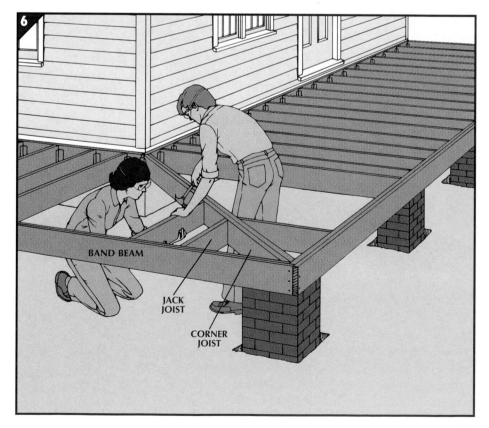

BAND BEAM

JACK JOIST

CORNER JOIST

LAYING FLOORBOARDS

1. Installing the outer rows.

◆ Cut the grooved edge from boards for the first row on one of the porch wings. Paint the cut edges with wood preservative.

◆ Starting where the wings meet, nail the first row of boards to the band beam, tongued edges toward the house, with $2\frac{1}{2}$-inch galvinized finishing nails every 16 inches. Position the boards so that their cut edges overhang the band beam by $1\frac{1}{2}$ inches, and allow the two end boards to overhang the corners about 3 inches.

◆ Trim the next few rows of boards so that their ends meet over joists, randomizing the joints. Before nailing a row of boards in place, measure their distance from the house wall at several points. Adjust the tongue-and-groove joint to make the boards parallel to the wall. Then tongue-nail each board in the row to every joist (page 13, inset).

2. Using a power nailer.

When you have installed at least 4 rows of boards, speed up the installation by using a power floor nailer. Continue to measure the distance between the boards and the house wall every few rows to be sure they are still parallel. Do not install the last 3 rows against the house.

3. Mitering floorboards at the corner.

◆ Tack a straight board to the floor parallel to the corner joist to serve as a saw guide. Position the guide so that the saw cuts the boards at the seam in the 2-piece joist.

◆ Install flooring for the second wing, precutting 45° angles on board ends that abut the first wing (page 27).

◆ Precut and install the last 3 rows of boards on both wings. Nail through the face of each board into the joists below, taking care not to pierce the ledger flashing. If necessary, trim the last row of boards lengthwise to fit under the siding.

◆ Trim the boards at the end of each wing, leaving a $1\frac{3}{4}$-inch overhang.

◆ Sink exposed nailheads; fill the holes with wood putty.

The All-Important Stairway

To do a large porch justice, a stairway should be wide enough to span the distance between the centers of two piers. For solidity underfoot, plan to install the carriages that support the steps no more than 30 inches apart. Although dimensions can vary, a stairway with carriages cut for steps 7 to 8 inches high and 10 inches deep are the safest and most comfortable to climb.

Getting Ready: Have on hand all the materials you need before beginning the job. In all likelihood, you will have to not only crosscut tread stock—$1\frac{1}{4}$-by-12 lumber with one edge rounded—and risers to length but also rip them to width. Coat with wood preservative any lumber that is not pressure treated. Plan to install the carriages and blocking within 48 hours of pouring the concrete base for the stairs.

 MATERIALS

2-by-2s
2-by-12s
$1\frac{1}{4}$-inch tread
  stock
1-inch fascia and riser
  stock
$1\frac{5}{8}$-inch lath
Wood lattice

1. Positioning the base.
◆ Mark the total run of the stairway on top of a mason's level with tape.
◆ Butt the level against the band beam under the flooring, and hold a folding ruler perpendicular to the level at the tape. Set the level aside and chalk an X where the ruler touches the ground. Connect this mark and two others made the same way with a line the width of the stairway, then outline a trench 2 inches in front of the line, 12 inches behind it, and 6 inches beyond each end.
◆ Dig the trench 4 inches deep and fill it with concrete to grade *(page 31)*.
◆ Recalculate the total rise from the concrete surface and make any necessary adjustments in riser height.

2. Making the carriages.
◆ Mark a 2-by-12 with the unit rise and unit run —7 inches and 10 inches in this case—as shown on page 31, making the bottom riser shorter than the others by the thickness of the tread stock. Draw the carriage-back line as shown at right.
◆ Cut out the carriage and check the fit. Remake the piece if the distance between the top tread and the surface of the porch floor is not exactly equal to the thickness of the tread stock.
◆ Use the carriage as a template for the others.

3. Attaching the carriages.

◆ Cut 8 pieces of blocking from joist stock to fit between carriages when they are evenly spaced across the width of the stairway.

◆ Rest the center carriage against the band beam. Nail a piece of blocking to the band beam so that the blocking touches the carriage, then nail through the carriage into the blocking. Fasten another length of blocking to the band

beam to sandwich the center carriage.

◆ Working from the center outward, anchor the tops of the remaining carriages to blocking.

◆ At the bottom of the stairway, set blocking between an end carriage and an adjacent one. Nail the blocking to the concrete base with $2\frac{1}{2}$-inch masonry nails, then fasten the carriages to the blocking. Install the remaining three pieces of blocking.

4. Adding risers and treads.

◆ From 1-inch stock, cut risers to fit as shown above, and fasten them with $3\frac{1}{2}$-inch galvanized finishing nails.

◆ Trim tread stock for a 1-inch overhang at the front and sides of each step; nail the treads to the carriages.

◆ Make fascia boards from 1-inch lumber, mitering the ends at porch corners for a finished appearance. Attach the fascia to the band beam with galvanized finishing nails.

◆ Cover the seam between the fascia and carriages with ogee molding.

◆ Countersink all nailheads and fill the holes with wood putty.

SKIRTS TO HIDE A CRAWLSPACE

Constructing lattice screens.

◆ Build a 2-by-2 frame to fit between adjacent piers. Nail a section of prefabricated lattice to the frame, then trim the lattice flush. Cover lattice edges with strips of $1\frac{5}{8}$-inch lath.

◆ Attach 2-by-4 furring strips to the sides of the brick piers with masonry nails driven into mortar joints. Position the furring strips so the screen fits snugly against the inner face of the overhanging fascia.

◆ Nail the lattice frame to the furring strips and the fascia.

◆ Countersink all exposed nailheads and fill the holes with wood putty.

◆ Adapt this procedure to make triangular-shaped lattice screens for the sides of the stairway.

A Hip Roof for a Wraparound Porch

The real trick to roof framing is cutting rafters—common and jack rafters for the wings and a hip rafter at the corner. There is more to these angled boards than meets the eye. The main challenge is to cut a notch called a bird's mouth where the outer end of the rafter rests on a header that supports the roof at the eaves.

The Ideal Pitch: For a porch of a given width, the location and depth of the bird's mouth depend primarily on the pitch of the roof. Most porch roofs have the same slope as the roof of the house they are attached to. To measure the slope of an existing roof, adapt the technique on page 64, Step 1 to measure the number of inches rise per foot of run, a figure called the unit rise.

Because a porch roof may approach second-story window sills no closer than 3 inches, you may have to settle for a gentler slope. The box opposite explains how to predict this outcome, once you know the dimensions of the rafter stock you need. For a porch up to 8 feet wide use 2-by-6s. Porches between 8 feet and 11 feet wide demand 2-by-8s.

Adjusting Pitch: Decrease the slope if the ideal pitch brings the roof too close to second-story windows. Roofing materials impose limits on this reduction. With a unit rise of 4 or more you may use any material you like—tile, slate, cedar shakes, or asphalt shingles. But a unit rise of 3 disqualifies all but asphalt shingles. Shallower slopes require a built-up roof. Consider lowering the porch-ceiling height—8 feet is standard— slightly to meet the 3-inch limit—or consult a roofer.

Lumber Sizes: Use common-rafter stock for the header, joists, ledger boards, and jack rafters. The hip rafter at the corner and rafter plates attached to the house require boards 2 inches wider.

Porch posts are generally 4-by-4s, but if piers are more than 9 feet apart, use 6-by-6s.

TOOLS
Framing square
Plumb bob
Circular saw
Carpenter's level
Handsaw or saber saw

MATERIALS
2-by-4s
2-by-6s, 2-by-8s, or 2-by-10s
1-by-6s or 1-by-8s
Plywood ($\frac{1}{2}$-inch)
Lag screws ($\frac{1}{2}$- by 3$\frac{1}{2}$-inch and $\frac{3}{8}$- by 5-inch)
Joist hangers
Framing, post, and
rafter anchors
15-pound roofing felt and nails
Aluminum drip edge
Asphalt shingles
Ridge venting
Aluminum flashing
Self-sealing roofing nails
Galvanized common nails (1$\frac{1}{2}$-, 2$\frac{1}{2}$-, and 3-inch)
Gutters and downspouts

Anatomy of a wraparound porch roof.

Joists and sloping boards called common rafters form the skeleton of a porch roof. The corner is shaped by a hip rafter and shorter jack rafters, elements mimicked by a corner joist and jack joists below them. Joists and rafters are anchored at one end to plates fastened to the house wall, and at the other to a header supported by posts centered over brick piers. Asphalt shingles laid over roofing felt and $\frac{1}{2}$-inch plywood sheathing keep out the weather. At the rafter plate, a strip of venting material covered by aluminum flashing promotes air circulation between rafters and joists. A tongue-and-groove ceiling hides the joists. Horizontal boards called lookouts give a nailing surface for the ceiling along the eaves and for the fascia.

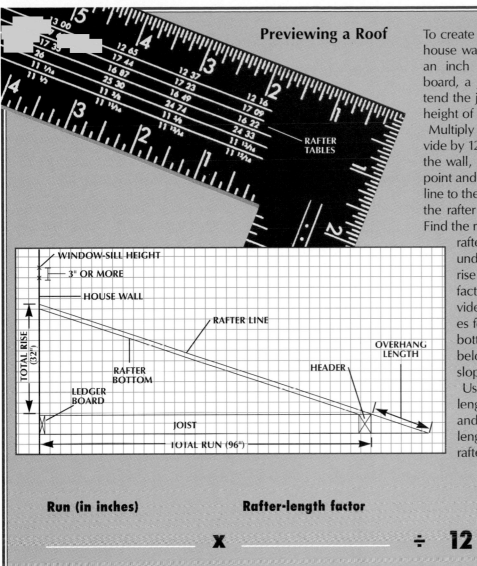

Previewing a Roof

RAFTER TABLES

WINDOW-SILL HEIGHT
3" OR MORE
HOUSE WALL
RAFTER LINE
TOTAL RISE (32")
OVERHANG LENGTH
RAFTER BOTTOM
HEADER
LEDGER BOARD
JOIST
TOTAL RUN (96")

To create the planning diagram at left, draw the house wall on 12-to-the-inch graph paper. Half an inch above ceiling height, add a ledger board, a joist, and a $3\frac{1}{2}$-inch-wide header. Extend the joist bottom to the right, and mark the height of second-story windows on the wall.

Multiply unit rise by total run in inches, then divide by 12 to get total rise. Mark this distance on the wall, up from the ledger's top. Through this point and the corner of the header, draw a rafter line to the extended joist. Indicate the bottom of the rafter with a line parallel to the rafter line. Find the rafter-length factor in the top line of the rafter table on a framing square *(left, top)*, under the unit-rise inch mark. For a unit rise of 4, the factor is 12.65. Multiply the factor by the width of your rafters and divide by 12. Mark this distance plus 2 inches for roofing on the wall above the rafter bottom. If this point is less than 3 inches below the window sill, decrease roof slope or lower the porch ceiling.

Use the formula below to find the rafter length, then measure the overhang run and use it in the formula to find overhang length. Add the two lengths, and buy rafter stock longer than the sum.

Run (in inches)		Rafter-length factor			Rafter length
_____	x	_____	÷	12 =	_____

THE CORRECT HEIGHT FOR A RAFTER PLATE

HEADER THICKNESS
12"
4"

RAFTER-LINE DEPTH

Positioning a rafter line.

Before erecting the rafter plate, determine how much of the width of a rafter will lie above the theoretical roof rise.

◆ Set a framing square on a board of common-rafter stock and align the unit run on the outside of the body—12—and the unit rise—in this case 4—on the outer edge of the

tongue with the edge of the board as shown *(above, left)*. Starting at the 12, draw a line of a length equal to the thickness of the header—$3\frac{1}{2}$ inches in this example.

◆ Place the square as shown above, and measure the vertical distance from the top edge of the board to the end of the slanted line. This is the rafter-line depth.

SUPPORTS FOR THE ROOF

1. Snapping chalk lines for plates.

◆ For each wing of the porch, snap two plumb chalk lines on the house wall—one 3 inches in from the end of the wing, the other near the house corner. Snap a horizontal chalk line 8 feet, $\frac{1}{2}$ inch above the porch floor to mark the bottom of the ledger board, then add a line to mark the top of the ledger board.

◆ Measure up from this line a distance equal to the sum of the total rise and the rafter-line depth *(page 67)*—plus 2 inches to allow for roofing materials. Snap a horizontal chalk line at this height. Two inches plus the width of the rafter plate lower on the wall, snap another.

◆ Remove the siding at the ledger-board and rafter-plate positions *(page 38)*.

◆ Cut ledgers and rafter plates to overlap at the corner, and attach them to floor framing *(page 39)* or fasten them to studs in the wall with lag screws. Set the bottom edge of the rafter plate against the bottom of the opening in the siding.

2. Installing post anchors.

◆ On each wing, snap a chalk line along the floor, directly above the outer face of the band beam. Set post anchors at the lines *(inset)*: 3 inches in from the end of each wing, one at the intersection of chalk lines above the large corner pier, and one above the center of each noncorner pier.

◆ Place an offset washer in the base of each anchor, and mark the washer hole on the floor. Drill a $\frac{5}{16}$-inch hole 5 inches deep through the floor into the band beam.

◆ Fasten each anchor to the porch with a 5- by $\frac{3}{8}$-inch lag screw. Set a post support in each anchor.

3. Erecting posts.

◆ Set a post, slightly taller than porch-ceiling height, in the anchor at the end of one wing; brace it plumb with scrap 2-by-4s.

◆ Tack a joist to the end of the ledger board. While a helper holds the board level, mark the position of its bottom edge on the post. Take down the post and the joist. Similarly, mark a post for the outer end of the other porch wing. Cut and compare the two posts. If they are the same length, cut all of the posts to that length. Otherwise, custom measure and cut each post.

◆ Nail a post-and-beam connector to the top of each post except the one at the corner, then set each post in its anchor and drive nails partway through the anchor and into the wood. Brace the posts plumb with 2-by-4s.

4. Installing headers.

◆ Cut a pair of joist-stock boards to fit between the outside edge of one wing's end post and the middle of the adjacent post. Put a piece of $\frac{1}{2}$-inch plywood between the boards, and nail the assembly every 8 inches on alternate sides with three 3-inch nails. Make other headers to fit between the centers of adjacent posts, ending at the last post before the corner.

◆ Set the headers atop the posts, and nail them to the post connectors; toenail the abutting ends of adjacent headers together. Install headers on the other wing.

◆ For the corner, build header sections long enough to extend across the top of the corner post, then miter the ends of the headers at a 45° angle (inset); nail the headers to each other and toenail them to the post.

5. Squaring the frame.

◆ Tack a 2-by-4 to the ledger board and the header (above). Lay a second 2-by-4 on the first and tack one end 4 feet along the ledger board to make a diagonal brace for the header. Remove the braces installed at the end post in Step 3 (left).

◆ Mark the header and the floor 1 foot from the end post, then use a plumb line to align the marks. Nail the diagonal brace to the 2-by-4 linking the ledger board and header. Add a second brace at the midpoint of the

wing. Steady the other wing in the same way, then finish the nailing begun in Step 3 to secure the posts to the anchors.

◆ Beginning 4 inches from the corner of the house, install ceiling joists every 16 inches along each wing, attaching them with joist hangers. Remove header braces as you approach them. Toenail end joists to the ledger and header. Install corner joists and jack joists as for a floor (page 62, Steps 4 and 5). When all joists are in place, remove the remaining post braces.

CUTTING AND INSTALLING COMMON RAFTERS

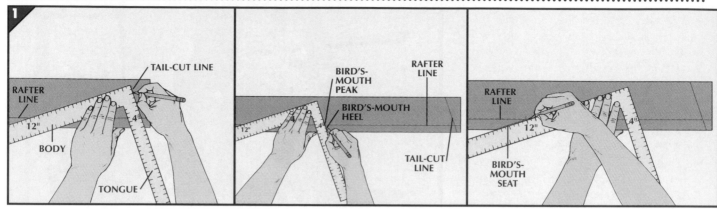

1. Marking tail and bird's-mouth cuts.

◆ With a chalk line, snap a rafter line along a rafter board at the depth established on page 67.
◆ Place a framing square near one end of the board, with the 12 on the body and the unit rise on the tongue touch-ing the rafter line. Draw a line along the tongue, then extend it across the board to establish the tail-cut line *(above, left)*.
◆ Measuring from the tail-cut line, mark the overhang length on the rafter line to establish the peak of the bird's mouth. Set the unit-rise number at the peak and the 12 on the rafter line, and draw the heel of the bird's mouth —a line from the peak to the bottom edge of the rafter *(above, center)*. Next, set the 12 at the peak and the unit-rise number on the rafter line, and draw the seat of the bird's mouth *(above, right)*.

2. Establishing the ridge cut.

◆ Mark the rafter length, measured from the bird's-mouth peak, on the rafter line. Place the unit-rise number on the framing square at the rafter-length mark and the 12 on the rafter line, then draw a ridge line along the tongue *(far left)*.
◆ To adjust rafter length for rafter-plate thickness, lay the tongue's inner edge along the ridge line as shown at left and mark two points $1\frac{1}{2}$ inches from the ridge line. Draw the ridge-cut line through the points.

3. Testing the rafter for fit.

◆ Make the ridge cut and the tail cut on the rafter with a circular saw. Use a saber saw or a handsaw to cut the bird's mouth.
◆ With a helper holding the rafter flush with the face and the end of the rafter plate, set the bird's mouth on the header. Recut the rafter if you find any gaps greater than $\frac{1}{8}$ inch at the rafter plate or bird's mouth *(the tip of the rafter may be higher than the top edge of the rafter plate)*. When you have a rafter that fits properly, use it as a tem-plate for the remaining common rafters *(inset)*.

4. Installing common rafters.

◆ Use a plumb bob to help mark the rafter plate directly above the side of each joist facing the porch corner, except for the two joists nearest the corner. For them, mark the plates $1\frac{1}{2}$ inches from the corner.

◆ At each rafter position, nail a multi-purpose framing anchor to the rafter plate so that it will not intrude between plate and rafter. Fasten wing-shaped rafter anchors to the header to meet the opposite face of each rafter.

◆ Attach each rafter to the plate and the header, nailing into the rafter face through the framing anchor and through the wing-shaped rafter anchor at the header *(inset)*.

ADDING HIP AND JACK RAFTERS

RIDGE LINE

RAFTER-
LINE DEPTH
MINUS $\frac{1}{4}$"

TAIL-CUT LINE

TAIL LINE

RIDGE-CUT
LINE

BIRD'S-MOUTH
SEAT

BIRD'S-
MOUTH HEEL

1. Making a hip rafter.

◆ Find the length of the hip rafter and its overhang with the formula on page 67. Use common-rafter total run and overhang run in the calculation, but consult the second line of the framing square's rafter table for the reference number.

◆ With a chalk line, snap a rafter line along the rafter board at the depth from the rafter's top edge established on page 67, less $\frac{1}{4}$ inch to compensate for roof sheathing. Using the number 17 on the body of the square, draw the tail line, the bird's mouth, and the ridge line on the rafter *(page 70, Step 1)*.

◆ For the ridge cut, adjust the ridge line *(page 70, Step 2)* by $3\frac{5}{8}$ inches instead of $1\frac{1}{2}$ inches to compensate for the thickness of the rafter-plate corner. Apply the same procedure to draw a tail-cut line $\frac{3}{4}$ inch closer to the bird's mouth than the tail line. Extend the tail- and ridge-cut lines across the top

and bottom edges of the rafter board with a try square, then connect these lines on the other face of the board.

◆ Cut out the bird's mouth with a saber saw. Set a circular saw at 45° and trim the rafter board along the ridge- and tail-cut lines on both faces to form V-shaped ends on the rafter.

◆ Install the hip rafter by nailing through the common rafters into the ridge end of the hip rafter, then toe-nailing it to the header.

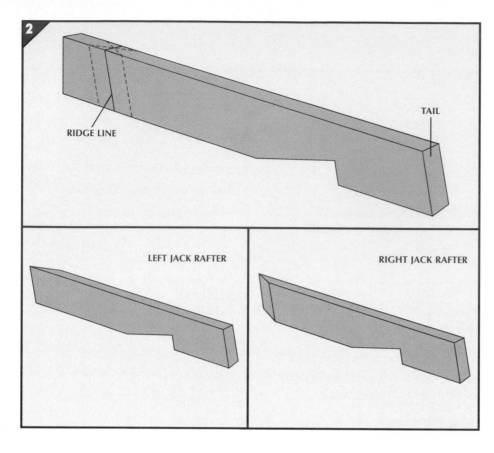

RIDGE LINE

TAIL

LEFT JACK RAFTER

RIGHT JACK RAFTER

2. Cutting the first jack rafters.

◆ Find the length in inches of the two shortest jack rafters under the unit-rise number in the third line of the rafter table, and add to it the overhang length of a common rafter. On boards slightly longer than this sum, mark rafter-line depth, then cut a bird's mouth and the rafter tail cut—all as for a common rafter *(pages 67 and 70)*. Locate and draw the ridge line *(left, top)* at rafter length minus $1\frac{1}{8}$ inches— half the diagonal thickness of the hip rafter—from the peak of the bird's mouth.

◆ On the rafter destined for the left side of the hip rafter, adjust the ridge line away from the tail $\frac{3}{4}$ inch *(blue dotted line)* as shown on page 70, Step 2. On the right-side joist, move the ridge line $\frac{3}{4}$ inch toward the tail *(red dotted line)*.

◆ Set a circular saw at 45° and make the ridge cuts for each side of the hip rafter as shown at left, bottom.

3. Installing the jack rafters.

◆ Cut the remaining jack rafters using one of the short jacks as a template for the tail and bird's-mouth cuts. Mark and cut the ridge bevels as in Step 2, increasing the length of each successive rafter by the number under the unit rise on the third line of the rafter table on the framing square.

◆ Starting with the shortest jack rafters, install each pair in succession, taking care not to bow the hip rafter. Face-nail the jacks to the hip rafter and attach them to the header with rafter anchors.

SHEATHING AND SHINGLES

1. A foundation for shingles.
◆ Lay sheets of Type C-D $\frac{1}{2}$-inch plywood horizontally, C side up, overhanging the rafter tails by $\frac{3}{4}$ inch and the end rafters by 3 inches. Leave $\frac{1}{16}$-inch—$\frac{1}{8}$-inch in very humid climates—expansion gaps between courses. Trim sheets so the ends rest on rafters and the joints of successive courses are staggered. Nail the plywood to the rafters with $1\frac{1}{2}$-inch nails, spacing the nails 6 inches apart at joints and 1 foot apart elsewhere. At the porch corner, trim the sheets for a $\frac{1}{8}$-inch gap at the center of the hip rafter. Leave a 1-inch ventilation opening between the top edge of the sheathing and the rafter plate.
◆ Unroll 15-pound roofing felt even with bottom edge of the plywood and tack the felt to the sheathing every few feet with wide-headed paper nails, ending 1 foot past the hip. Lay succeeding courses of felt to overlap earlier ones by 2 inches.
◆ Along the eave line, install an aluminum drip edge (inset). Secure it with roofing nails driven every foot.

⚠ **CAUTION** *Install temporary 2-by-4 footholds for added security when working on the roof.*

ROOFING FELT

DRIP EDGE

STARTER STRIP

ADHESIVE   TRIM LINE

TAB

2. Laying the first row of shingles.
◆ Trim the tabs from a section of roofing to make a starter strip (inset), then cut 6 inches from one end. Lay the strip in the corner formed by the drip edge and the end of a wing, then fasten it with three roofing nails along the center. Cut and lay full-length starter strips end to end along the eaves.
◆ Lay the first row of shingles on top of the starter course, overhanging porch-wing ends by $\frac{1}{2}$ inch. Fasten each section with $1\frac{1}{4}$-inch roofing nails driven $\frac{5}{8}$ inch above the slots that divide the strip into tabs. Place a nail above each slot and 1 inch from each end. At the corner, trim the shingles along the hip rafter.

3. Working up the roof.
◆ Shorten by 6 inches—half a tab—the first section of shingles in each successive course. Align the cut end with the end of the first shingle in the previous course, adjusting overlap to match the house roof. If the tab at the hip will be shorter than 6 inches, cut half a tab from the preceding section of shingles before laying the last section next to it.
◆ Adjust shingle overlap on the last few courses, if necessary, so that the top row will be at least 6 inches wide. Trim the shingles along the top edge of the sheathing.

4. Adding hip shingles.

◆ Make hip shingles by cutting shingle sections into three pieces at the slots, then rounding the upper ends *(inset)*. Fold one shingle down the center and set it at the eave line, then place another folded shingle at the house wall. With the aid of a helper, snap chalk lines down both sides of the hip to mark the edges of the hip shingles.

◆ Beginning at the eave, lay folded shingle tabs between the chalk lines, matching the overlap on the hip of the house roof. Fasten the shingles with a nail on each side, 2 inches above the spots of adhesive on each tab and 1 inch in from the edge.

5. Venting and flashing.

◆ Nail a strip of venting material along the top edge of the roof as shown above, following the manufacturer's instructions.

◆ Install aluminum flashing over the venting material *(inset)*. Buy flashing wide enough to extend 4 inches under the house siding and 1 inch beyond the venting material.

◆ Nail the flashing through the venting material and shingles, and into the roof sheathing at 1-foot intervals. Use self-sealing roofing nails, which are fitted with silicone or neoprene washers.

⚠ **CAUTION** *Overhammering the nails will crush the venting material.*

74

SIDE ENCLOSURES AND SOFFIT SUPPORTS

1. Installing lookouts.

◆ Use a level to mark the tail of each rafter flush with the bottom edge of the header, then saw the rafter along the line. Cut 2-by-4 lookouts to fit against the header and even with each rafter tail.

◆ Set the lower edge of the lookout flush with the bottom of the header and the newly cut edge at the rafter overhang. Face-nail the lookout to the rafter, then toenail it to the header *(top inset)*.

◆ Cut a lookout for each side of the hip rafter *(bottom inset)*, making parallel 45° bevels on both ends. Fit the lookouts to the header and hip rafter as in the bottom inset.

LOOKOUT

2. Enclosing the ends of the roof.

END RAFTER

RAKE BOARD

◆ Cut a piece of ½-inch exterior-grade plywood to cover the triangular space created by the rafter and the joist at the end of each wing. Extend the plywood ½ inch below the bottom of the joist to cover the ends of ceiling boards *(page 77)*. Nail the plywood cover to the rafter and the joist.

◆ From a 1-inch board the same width as a rafter, cut a rake board that matches the common rafters both in length and in the angle of the ridge and tail cuts. Butt the rake against the underside of the plywood sheathing and nail it to the plywood cover. If the plywood sheathing on the roof extends past the outer face of the rake, trim the corner with a strip of quarter-round molding.

3. Adding a fascia and gutters.

◆ Make fascia boards from 1-inch lumber about 2 inches wider than the depth of rafter tails. Cut the boards so that joints fall at the centers of the tails.

◆ Slip the fascia into the space between the tails and the drip edge, lining up the outer end of the fascia with the outer face of the rake board. Nail the fascia to the rafter tails. At the corner where the two wings meet, miter the ends of the fascia board at a 45° angle.

◆ Attach gutters to the fascia and downspouts to the corner post and end posts according to the manufacturer's instructions *(inset)*.

RAKE

FASCIA

RAKE

DRIP EDGE

Ceilings and Railings

Ceilings and railings, the finishing touches to a porch, are made of specially milled lumber called porch stock. For ceilings, it consists of tongue-and-groove boards $\frac{1}{2}$ inch thick and 3 inches wide with a bead down the center. These are generally installed from the house wall to the eaves, forming one continuous surface *(below)*.

To allow air to circulate within the enclosed space above the ceiling, screened vents are installed in the ceiling boards of the overhang. The vents are available in several shapes and sizes at hardware stores; your local building code will specify the correct size and spacing for your area.

Wood for Railings: Cap-rail stock for the upper railing is milled with a 1-inch-wide groove on the underside to accept the tops of 1-by-1 pickets. The picket bottoms fit against the angled face of bottom-rail stock as shown on the facing page. All three elements can be purchased specially milled for decorative effect, but they also come in the standard stock shown here, available in 16-foot lengths that can be cut to fit any porch.

MATERIALS

Ceiling boards
4-by-4s
Parting bead
Vents
Cap-rail stock
Bottom-rail stock
Pickets
Post caps
Ogee molding

A tongue-and-groove porch ceiling.

◆ Starting at the wall of the house, face-nail tongue-and-groove boards to the ceiling joists with 2-inch finishing nails. Where the two wings meet, miter the ceiling boards to join at a 45° angle. At the ends of the porch, butt the ceiling boards against the inside of the plywood triangle that encloses the roof. Notch the ceiling boards to fit around porch posts.

◆ Finish the ceiling by nailing flat molding such as parting bead around the perimeter of the ceiling to conceal ceiling board joints with the plywood triangles and fascia boards.

◆ Cut holes in the ceiling at the center of the overhang for placement of screened vents *(inset)*.

◆ Before painting, set all nails and fill the holes with putty.

POST CAP

CAP RAIL

GROOVE

PICKET

ANGLED FACE

BOTTOM RAIL

OGEE MOLDING

A railing to surround the porch.

◆ Between porch posts, install 4-by-4 railing posts cut 2 inches longer than the height of the railing as specified by building codes. Mount the uprights on post anchors, placing one post flush against the house at the end of each wing. Install others between porch posts as required by code. Cover the post anchors with 1-by-4 lumber finished with $\frac{1}{2}$-inch ogee molding, and top each post with a post cap.

◆ Toenail the bottom rails to the posts above the molding and with the angled face toward the house, then toenail cap rails to the posts.

◆ Cut a 1-by-1 picket to fit between the rails, mitering one end to the angle of the bottom rail (inset). Use the first picket as a template for marking others. Drill pilot holes to prevent splitting, then toenail the pickets to the rails so that the gaps between pickets are less than 4 inches wide.

A railing for the porch stairs.

◆ Cut posts for the bottom of the stairs to the same height as the other railing posts (left), and fasten them with post anchors to the concrete footing directly against each side of the bottom step, notching the bottom tread as needed. Cover the anchor with trim.

◆ Miter the bottom and cap rails to fit snugly between the posts at the top and bottom of the stairs.

◆ Cut pickets as for the porch railing, then miter the tops and bottoms to match the slope of the railing (inset). Toenail the pickets into place.

Classical Columns for Purists

A porch on a large house can benefit from posts that are more substantial in appearance than the basic 4-by-4 supports. The simplest to add are the hollow variety that enclose existing posts (left). Available from most large lumberyards in lengths from 8 to 20 feet, they can be ordered made of wood or aluminum, with plain or fluted columns, and topped with a choice of capitals, including some styled after ancient Greek architecture (right). All such columns come split in half for ease of installation.

Columns require weatherproofing whether made of aluminum or wood. Coat the inside with roofing compound to a height of 2 feet. Ventilate the column with two holes in the porch ceiling, one inside the column, the other within 1 foot of the exterior. If the capital protrudes past the fascia, install a strip of aluminum flashing to deflect rain.

IONIC

CORINTHIAN

Patios of Brick and Concrete

Masonry surfaces actually float on the surface of the ground, rising and subsiding with spring thaws and winter frosts. In the case of concrete, the slab floats on a layer of gravel, while bricks and stone embedded in sand shift individually to adapt to changing contours. Either structure requires considerable excavation, heavy work lightened by a rotary tiller used to loosen soil for easier removal.

A patio with a surface of bricks or concrete paving blocks is weather-resistant and enduring. Because the brick or concrete pavers are small and uniform in size, such a patio is also easy to install and maintain.

The Spectrum of Materials: Standing water and changing temperatures are tough on brick patios; buy paving bricks, which are stronger than those used to build vertical structures. As shown opposite, you can combine them in a number of patterns. Molded concrete paving blocks, on the other hand, are designed to interlock.

Choosing Sand or Concrete: Both brick and concrete pavers may be set on a tightly compacted bed of sand *(pages 82-87)* or on a concrete slab with mortar *(page 103)*. Sand is self-draining and lets the pavers move independently as the earth shifts, and pavers set on sand can be leveled or replaced individually. Patios of mortared bricks or blocks, however, last longer, need less upkeep, and rarely have weeds.

Maintaining the Patio: Whether the pavers are on sand or concrete, moss may be a problem. Although it can be attractive, moss can also be a slippery hazard. To eliminate it, apply moss killer, sold at garden-supply stores. If your patio develops mildew stains, scrub it with household bleach. Finally, weeds can grow between pavers laid on sand, even when a weed-control barrier has been placed underneath. If that happens, you may need to spray all gaps with herbicide, taking care not to spray near trees and other desirable plants.

SAFETY TIPS

Wear hard-toed shoes when you are transporting brick or concrete pavers. If you are working with mortar, leather-palmed work gloves will protect your hands from irritants.

PAVERS FOR PATIOS

Brick pavers.
The paving brick at near right measures about $3\frac{5}{8}$ inches wide by $7\frac{5}{8}$ inches long; these dimensions allow for ample mortar joints between bricks. You can also purchase paving bricks like the one above it, which is exactly twice as long as it is wide. For use on a sand bed, these bricks fit together without gaps to help keep weeds from poking through. In climates where the ground freezes, use paving bricks that are rated SX, which means they can withstand severe weather.

Concrete pavers.
Molded concrete paving blocks come in numerous shapes; the three shown at right are among the more common. Because the blocks are laid down in interlocking patterns, they are less likely to shift position during or after installation.

4″ x 8″

$3\frac{5}{8}″$ x $7\frac{5}{8}″$

STACK BOND

RUNNING BOND

BASKET WEAVE

HERRINGBONE

An emphasis on regularity. You can set rectangular bricks in any of the four classic patterns shown above, or combine the patterns to give varied surface designs. Avoid the stack-bond arrangement for large patios, since it is difficult to align; instead, frame other patterns with a stack-bond border. A running-bond pattern, in which the bricks are staggered, is easier to lay uniformly over a broad area.

Interlocking patterns like basket weave and herringbone, in which brick orientation varies, increase the durability of a sand-bed patio, since each brick is held in place by its neighbors. The basket weave above has brick faces exposed; another version has the bricks set on their sides, three to a square. Herringbone, with its directional nature, is useful for directing a viewer's eye to a particular spot.

Layouts based on circles.

To accommodate a tree, a fountain, or other fixed object, lay a circular pattern *(far left).* Begin at the center with two rings of half bricks, then add rings of full-size bricks to fill an area of any size *(page 86).*

A scalloped effect like that used on European boulevards *(near left)* is achieved with overlapping arcs of brick as shown on page 87. Loosely fill the scallops with whole and half bricks.

By far the easiest patio to build is one made of bricks set into a bed of sand. A sand base allows rainwater to seep down to tree or shrub roots, and sand lets bricks accommodate the earth below as it settles or shifts with freezing and thawing.

When planning a patio, consider the stability of the ground. Recent landfill more than 3 feet deep or water found within 1 foot of the surface may cause settling problems. If such conditions exist—or if you live in an earthquake zone—consult a landscape architect.

Laying Out a Sand Bed: To minimize brick cutting, lay a dry run around the patio perimeter before excavating, adjusting the patio dimensions to incorporate as many whole bricks as possible. Be sure to plan for a permanent edging *(page 84)*, required to keep sand-laid bricks from shifting. Chop out tree roots near the surface that would prevent bricks from lying flat. Before digging, check with a building inspector to see if you must erect a silt fence to keep eroded soil on your property.

Drainage: Usually, 2 inches of sand on well-tamped earth offers adequate drainage. Dense clay soils or heavy rainfall, however, often require the added drainage of a 4-inch layer of gravel under the sand. Use the estimator on page 88 to figure the amounts you need. To prevent sand from sifting down into the gravel, cover it with 15-pound roofing felt or 6-mil polyethylene sheeting punctured to let rainwater through. If drainage is a

particular problem, slope the sand bed away from the house about 1 inch every 4 to 6 feet. Perforated drain tile or plastic tubing laid in the gravel layer helps drain water away from wet spots.

Choosing the Right Bricks: Untextured, exterior-grade bricks are best; rough or grooved surfaces collect water that can crack bricks when it freezes. But avoid glazed bricks, which become slippery when wet. "Bricks" of molded concrete, which come in a wide array of colors and shapes, offer an alternative to traditional clay brick.

With Gaps or Without: Patterns of bricks laid tight against one another control weeds better than bricks laid with gaps between them. For a gapless patio, buy special paving bricks exactly half as wide as they are long.

Other paving bricks are sized for mortar joints between them. The gap both accentuates the pattern and channels rainwater down the long side of the brick—away from the house, if you align the long edges with any slope the site may have. Plastic sheeting laid on the sand bed before the bricks are laid helps keep weeds from growing in the gaps, and sand swept into the gaps keeps the bricks from moving.

⚠ **CAUTION** *Before excavating, establish the locations of underground obstacles such as electric, water, and sewer lines, and dry wells, septic tanks, and cesspools.*

TOOLS

Brickset
4-pound maul
Mason's hammer
Rubber mallet
Level
Framing square
Circular saw with a carbide
    masonry blade

MATERIALS

Bricks
Washed gravel ($\frac{3}{4}$-inch)
Polyethylene sheeting
Sand
2-by-2 stakes
String

SAFETY TIPS

Wear eye protection when cutting bricks. A dust mask is recommended when trimming brick with a circular saw. Gloves help prevent blisters and abrasions.

TWO METHODS FOR CUTTING BRICKS

Using a brickset.
To cut a small number of bricks, use a wide chisel—called a brickset—and a 4-pound maul. Draw a cutting line on the brick, then cushion the brick on sand or a board. Hold the brickset vertically with the beveled edge facing away from you and strike the tool sharply. Then tilt the brickset slightly toward you and strike again, thus splitting the brick. Practice on a few broken bricks before you cut the bricks you will use.

Scoring bricks with a circular saw.
Large numbers of bricks are more easily cut with the help of a circular saw fitted with a carbide masonry blade. Hold the brick in a simple jig made of 2-by-4 scraps, spaced a brick's width apart and nailed to a piece of plywood. Set the saw for a $\frac{1}{4}$-inch cut, then slowly guide the blade along the cutting line, grooving the brick. Make a matching groove on the other side, then hold the brick in your hand and break off the unwanted portion with the blunt end of a mason's hammer *(inset)*.

EXCAVATING FOR A PATIO

Laying out a rectangular site.
◆ Drive reference nails into the wall of the house to mark both sides of the patio.
◆ Use the method shown on page 22 to establish positions for 2-by-2 stakes opposite the nails and 2 feet beyond the end of the future patio.
◆ Tie string between the nails and stakes to establish side boundary lines for the patio and mark each string where the patio will end.
◆ With a helper *(above)*, stake a third string so that it crosses the marks you made on the side boundary lines.
◆ To excavate the area, first dig a trench along the boundary lines. Make the trench deep enough to accommodate the bricks, sand, and gravel if any. Work in parallel rows, back and forth between the perimeter trenches.

Laying out an irregular shape.

◆ Draw the patio on graph paper, with each square representing 1 square foot. To estimate the area of the patio, assign a rough fractional value to parts of squares inside the outline. Then add up the full squares and the fractions. Use this figure when buying brick, sand, and gravel.

◆ Lay out a garden hose in the shape of the patio, then outline the perimeter on the ground with a dispenser of powdered chalk *(page 94)*. Trench around the perimeter, then excavate.

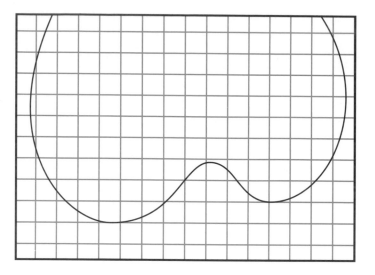

LAYING BRICKS IN SAND

1. Edging the perimeter.

◆ First, compact the earth inside the excavation with a tamper *(page 89)*.

◆ Around the perimeter, dig a narrow trench such that the top of a brick stood on end in the trench will be even with the patio surface. *(If a side of the patio will border a flower bed, let the edging extend 2 inches higher.)*

◆ Tamp the bottom of the trench with the end of a 2-by-4, then stretch reference strings as guides for aligning the tops of the edging bricks with one another. Next, stand bricks upright around the perimeter *(above)*, with their top edges touching the strings. Press earth against the bricks to hold them up.

◆ Add washed gravel as necessary, distributing it evenly over the surface with a rake. Cover the gravel with roofing felt, or polyethylene sheeting that has been punctured with drainage holes at 4- to 6-inch intervals.

◆ Spread a 2-inch layer of sand over the bed. Dampen the sand, then tamp the surface again.

Alternative edgings.

To make a sawtooth pattern with teeth protruding 2 inches above the patio surface *(above)*, set the bricks at an angle of 45° in the trench. Other choices for edgings include rot-resistant redwood or pressure-treated 2-by-6s *(above, right)* set in a narrower trench, or upright bricks set in a curve *(right)* for a rounded corner. To lay out a curved corner, use a level to align the tops of the bricks.

2. Laying the bricks.

◆ Use a reference string to help align bricks in the pattern you choose for your patio. Begin a herringbone pattern, for example, with a brick set at a 45° angle to the edging in each of two adjacent patio corners. Tap the bricks into the sand with a rubber mallet to make them flush with the edging bricks.

◆ Stretch a string between two spare bricks, set just outside the edging, so that the string passes over the corners of the two corner bricks. As you set bricks in the first row, align corners with the string. Use the mallet or adjust the sand bed to keep the bricks even with one another.

◆ To begin a new row, lay a brick at each end as a guide for positioning the reference string. Fill in the row, smoothing any sand you may have disturbed. Repeat for each row.

◆ Fill triangular spaces along the patio edges with brick that you have cut to fit, then gently sweep sand into any gaps that remain. Add more sand if necessary after it rains.

A CIRCULAR PATIO TO SURROUND A TREE

1. Starting with half bricks.

◆ Loop a garden hose around the tree to mark inner and outer perimeters for the patio. Make the inner circle at least 3 feet in diameter to avoid wide gaps between the half bricks used in the first two courses.

◆ Excavate and edge the area to be paved, then prepare the sand bed.

◆ Cut half bricks for the first course and tap them into place with a rubber mallet, wedging the inner corners of the bricks tight against each other *(left)*. Use a level to align the tops of the bricks. Trim the last half brick in each course as needed for a snug fit.

◆ Lay a second course of half bricks against the first.

2. Setting the whole bricks.

◆ Place concentric circles of whole bricks in the sand bed so that their inner edges touch at the corners and butt against the preceding course. Tap each brick into place with a rubber mallet. Use a 4-foot mason's level to align the brick, adding or removing sand as necessary.

◆ Continue laying whole bricks in concentric circles out to the edging.

3. Filling gaps at the edge.

◆ Mark a brick to fit each oddly shaped nook along the patio's outer perimeter. Cut the brick with a brickset as shown on page 83, then trim as needed by chipping it with the sharp end of a mason's hammer. Set the brick into place with a rubber mallet.

◆ Gently brush sand into the gaps between bricks, repeating the process as necessary to refill the cracks after a rain.

SETTING BRICKS IN OVERLAPPING SCALLOPS

1. Scribing scallop arcs.

◆ Use the edging of a sand bed to establish a base line for drawing semicircles in the sand. Arcs that have a radius of 24 inches and are spaced with their centers 60 inches apart make an attractive pattern. Scribe arcs across one end of the sand bed, with partial arcs at the sides if necessary.

◆ Stretch a string between two bricks so that it crosses the tops of the arcs in the first row *(above)*. Kneeling on boards to avoid disturbing arcs already drawn, scribe another row of arcs with centers midway between those in the first row. A framing square helps in marking these centers and those in subsequent rows. Use partial arcs in the last row if necessary.

2. Paving the scallops.

◆ Arrange whole bricks along each arc *(right)*, then with a partial brick, start filling each scallop at the narrow space between arcs. Half a brick, followed by three-quarters of a brick in the next course, works well with 24-inch arcs.

◆ Pave the rest of each scallop with whole bricks laid in slightly curving rows *(inset)*. Fill partial scallops with whole bricks and any cavities with cut bricks or sand.

◆ Sweep sand into any gaps that remain.

Groundwork for a Concrete Slab

A concrete slab consists of a layer of concrete, usually reinforced with wire mesh, that rests on a drainage bed of gravel. Although the 4-inch reinforced slab on 4 inches of gravel described on the following pages satisfies many building codes, always check with local authorities for the correct specifications.

Building codes may also specify the degree of slope required for water runoff and whether a silt fence is needed during construction to limit soil erosion. Local zoning laws may dictate the location, design, and size of a slab.

Getting Started: Selecting a site for a slab requires the same care as choosing one for a brick patio *(page 82)*. When your plan is completed use the estimator below to calculate how much concrete and gravel you'll use, based on the area of the slab and the thickness of the concrete plus the gravel bed.

To prepare the site for a rectangular slab, lay out boundaries with wood stakes and string as shown on page 83, and excavate the site. Dig 2 feet beyond the strings to accommodate form boards and

braces, then proceed as shown here. Site preparation for a free-form slab appears on pages 94-95. Save sod and dirt to fill in at the sides of the finished slab.

Expansion Joints: Many local codes require a strip of asphalt-impregnated expansion-joint filler in the concrete every 8 to 10 feet of a slab's length and between the slab and the house foundation *(page 92, Step 7)*. The purpose of the joints is to prevent damage as concrete expands and contracts with changes in temperature. Try to buy joint filler as wide as the thickness of the slab. If unavailable, somewhat narrower or wider filler is satisfactory.

Forms to Shape Concrete: Unless you plan on a decorative pattern of permanent form boards *(page 93)*, build forms from inexpensive woods such as fir, spruce, or pine. Plywood, made flexible with the technique shown on page 94, is used to mold the curves of a free-form slab. Double-headed nails allow both types of temporary forms to be quickly disassembled.

TOOLS

Common carpentry tools	Rake
Spade	4-pound maul
Tamper	Line level
Screed	Wire cutters

MATERIALS

1-by-2s	Masonry nails
2-by-4s	($1\frac{1}{2}$-inch)
Plywood ($\frac{3}{4}$-inch)	Washed gravel
2-by-2 stakes	($\frac{3}{4}$-inch)
Mason's cord	Expansion-joint filler
Double-headed nails (2-inch)	Reinforcing mesh
	Binding wire
Common nails (3-inch)	Concrete blocks
	Powdered chalk
Spikes (6-inch)	Lath

SAFETY TIPS

Wear goggles when nailing form boards together and joint filler to the house. Gloves protect your hands from blisters, splinters, and especially cuts when handling wire mesh.

CALCULATIONS FOR SLOPE AND VOLUME

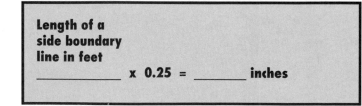

Length of a side boundary line in feet

_____ x 0.25 = _____ inches

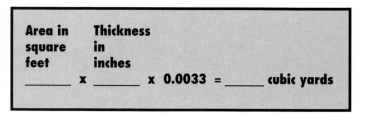

Area in square feet   Thickness in inches

_____ x _____ x 0.0033 = _____ cubic yards

Calculating slope.

For a slope of $\frac{1}{4}$ inch per foot, use the formula above to determine the difference in height between the edge of the slab that abuts the house and the edge parallel to it. Multiply by 0.125 instead of 0.25 for a slope of $\frac{1}{8}$ inch per foot.

Estimating cubic yardage.

Use the estimator above to find the amount of concrete or gravel needed for a slab or drainage bed. The result in cubic yards—the bulk measure in which such materials are sold—includes an 8 percent allowance for waste and spillage.

1. Leveling the excavated area.

◆ Using a rake, break up any clods of earth; then, with a helper, pull an 8-foot-long 2-by-4 leveling board across the area to smooth it (above).

◆ Dampen the area with a hose, and compact the surface by pounding it with a tamper. You can rent one or build one from a 2-foot square of $\frac{3}{4}$-inch plywood with a braced handle, 4 feet high, made of 2-by-4s.

◆ After tamping, pull the leveling board across the area again, using it as a straightedge to make sure that the surface is reasonably even.

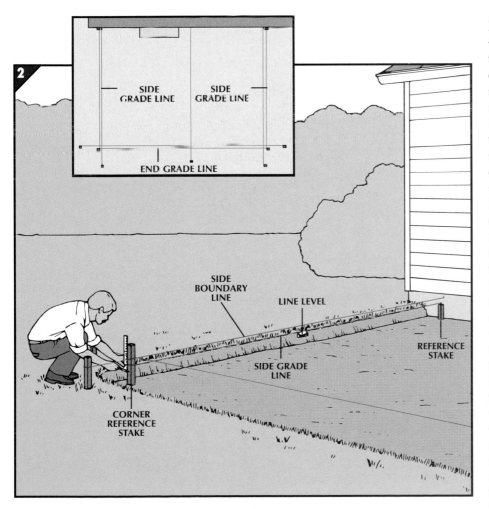

2. Establishing the grade.

◆ Mark the slab height—the sum of the slab and gravel-bed thicknesses—on the house wall, 2 inches outside a side boundary line. Center a 2-by-2 reference stake on the mark and drive it into the ground next to the house wall, bringing the top even with the slab-height mark. Center a nail on top of the stake and hammer it in partway.

◆ Measure along the side boundary line to a point 2 inches beyond the end boundary line, and drive a corner reference stake opposite the first. Loop a string around the second stake and tie it to the nail in the other. Hang a line level at the center of the string and adjust the string at the corner stake to make the string level.

◆ Use the formula on the preceding page to calculate slope, and mark the resulting distance on the corner stake, below the string. Lower the string to the mark, called a grade mark.

◆ Repeat for the other side of the slab.

◆ Connect the grade marks on the corner stakes with a third string to make an end grade line. Use that line and a reference stake near the house to establish a grade line within the slab for each expansion joint required.

3. Adding support stakes.
◆ Mark the grade lines at 2-foot intervals. Directly below each marker, drive a 2-by-2 form-support stake deep enough so you can't pull it out by hand and so the grade line just touch-es the top of the stake. Place stakes precisely to ensure that corners will be square and the slab sloped correctly.
◆ When all of the support stakes are in place, remove the grade lines and use a handsaw to trim the corner reference stakes to the height marked ear-lier for the grade lines. Then re-move all the boundary-marker strings and stakes; leave only the support stakes and the cor-ner reference stakes.

4. Installing form boards.
◆ Cut a 2-by-4 form board 4 inch-es longer than the distance from the house to the outer edge of the reference stake. Use more than one if needed, butting the boards.
◆ Set a board against the inside faces of the support stakes, one end against the house. Rest the board on wood blocks so that the top edge is even with the tops of the stakes.

◆ Drive a 2-inch double-headed nail through each end stake into the board, using a maul as an anvil *(above)*. Then nail the board to the intermediate stakes.
◆ Install a form board for the other side of the slab in the same way.
◆ Nail a form board for the end of the slab to its support stakes. Where this board abuts the side boards, toenail the joints with 3-inch common nails.

◆ For each expansion joint, cut a board $\frac{1}{2}$ inch shorter than the dis-tance between the house and the end board. Nail the board to its support stakes on the side of the slab that will be poured first, leav-ing a $\frac{1}{2}$-inch space at the wall.
◆ Where boards abut *(inset)*, drive a support stake 6 inches to each side of the joint. Nail the boards to the stakes, then nail a strip of $\frac{1}{2}$-inch plywood over the joint.

5. Bracing the form boards.

◆ Drive a support stake at the corners where end and side boards meet.
◆ Reinforce each support stake, including those flanking a joint, with a 1-by-2 brace nailed to a stake driven about 1 foot from the form board.
◆ Excavate the slab area along the end board to match the slope of the side form boards, then smooth and tamp.

END BOARD

CORNER SUPPORT STAKE

BRACING STAKES

BRACE

6. Screeding the gravel.

Pour a layer of $\frac{3}{4}$-inch gravel into each section of the slab, allowing it to spill out under the form boards. With a helper, smooth the gravel by dragging a screed across its surface.

TRICKS OF THE TRADE

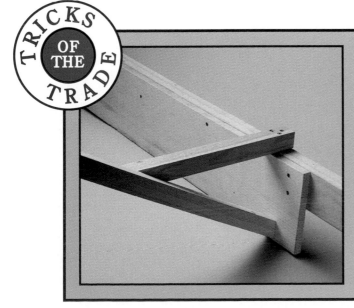

To Make a Screed

The function of a screed is to assure a smooth gravel surface and a uniform slab thickness. To make the screed shown here, which is designed for a slab 4 inches thick, cut a 1-by-8 board 2 inches shorter than the distance between forms, and a 2-by-4 board 10 inches longer than this distance. Center the 1-by-8 on the 2-by-4. Offset the 1-by-8 board $\frac{1}{4}$ inch and nail the boards together. To the face of the 1-by-8, toenail two 2-by-2 handles, each 4 feet long and cut at a 30° angle at one end. Brace the handles with 2-by-2s nailed to the top of the 2-by-4.

7. Installing joint filler.

◆ Cut a strip of expansion-joint filler the length of the expansion-joint form. Every foot or so, hammer 3-inch nails through one side of the filler and bend the points slightly to anchor it in the slab.

◆ Set the filler against the form *(above)*. Use 6-inch spikes, if necessary, to support the filler at the correct height, even with the top *(inset)*.

◆ Nail another strip of filler to the house wall with $1\frac{1}{2}$-inch masonry nails at 6-inch intervals, outlining any existing stairs. Butt the filler against the side form boards and work it into the $\frac{1}{2}$-inch space between expansion-joint forms and the house.

8. Laying wire mesh.

◆ Wearing gloves, unroll mesh over the gravel. Begin at the outer edge of the slab, and leave 2 inches between the mesh and the form boards. Weigh down the mesh with concrete blocks as you go. When you reach the other side of a section, use wirecutters to trim the mesh 2 inches short of the form board. Then turn the mesh over, and walk on it to flatten it.

◆ Cover the gravel in the section you intend to pour first, allowing panels of mesh to overlap 6 inches. Cut the mesh to fit around steps or other obstacles, then tie panels together with binding wire.

EXPANSION
JOINT

SECONDARY BOARDS

PRIMARY BOARD

PERIMETER BOARD

SUPPORT STAKE

2-BY-4 STAKE

THE APPEAL OF PERMANENT FORM BOARDS

In most instances, form boards become scrap lumber after a slab is poured. A decorative option, however, is to leave them in place as a frame around the slab or, as shown here, to lay out an attractive pattern of interior form boards. For this purpose, pressure-treated or other weather-resistant wood is superior to the pine or spruce used for temporary forms.

Installing permanent form boards follows the same principles used for setting up temporary boards—with a few differences. When laying out the perimeter for such a slab, take into account that the form boards will contribute to its length and width. Set up and brace perimeter form boards as shown on pages 90-91, but drive support stakes for interior boards as well as perimeter boards an inch below the planned surface of the slab so that the concrete will conceal them.

Establish the slope of the slab as shown on page 89. Each interior board that will lie perpendicular to the house needs a grade line. Boards oriented parallel to the house each require a string set up in the same way as an end line (page 89).

Permanent form boards replace expansion joints within the slab but not the one along the house. Boards that cross from one side of the slab to the other are called primary form boards. Next to the house use stakes to secure the ends of primary form boards; nail through perimeter form boards to secure other ends.

Secondary form boards are shorter than the width or length of the patio. Where secondary form boards meet perimeter or primary form boards, they can be face-nailed. Where two secondary boards meet, nail one to the other and toenail both to a 2-by-4 stake driven into the ground under the joint.

Before pouring the slab, drive 3-inch nails halfway into all the form boards to help anchor them in the concrete, and cover their top edges with heavy-duty tape to prevent concrete stains.

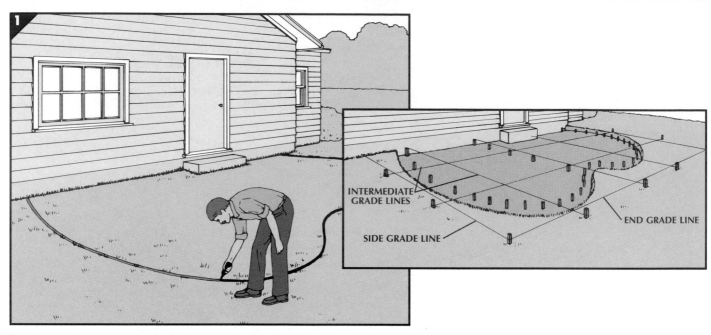

INTERMEDIATE GRADE LINES

SIDE GRADE LINE

END GRADE LINE

1. Excavating the slab area.

◆ Establish the slab shape with a garden hose, then mark the shape on the ground with powdered chalk.

◆ Remove the hose, and excavate the area a distance 2 feet beyond the chalk line. Dig to a depth equal to the thickness of the drainage bed plus the thickness of the slab. Dig back and forth across the area in parallel rows, then smooth and tamp the soil in the bottom of the excavation.

◆ Establish drainage away from the house, first by setting up boundary lines and grade lines for a rectangle a foot or two larger in each dimension than the slab's maximum length and width *(inset)*.

◆ Tie intermediate grade lines at 3-foot intervals between the side lines, and between the wall of the house and the end line; at the house, tie the strings to masonry nails.

◆ Drive 2-by-2 support stakes into the ground around the slab perimeter, 2 feet in from the edge of the excavation. Space the stakes 2 feet apart along gradual curves, 1 foot apart around sharp curves.

◆ Add support stakes for any interior forms required, spacing them at 2-foot intervals. Set the tops of the stakes even with the strings.

TRICKS OF THE TRADE

Taking the Stiffness Out of Plywood

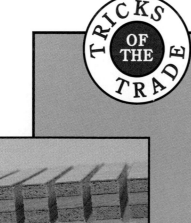

The rigidity of plywood—layers of wood glued together under pressure—results from orienting the grain in each layer perpendicular to the grain in its neighbors. Yet you can make even $\frac{3}{4}$-inch plywood bend enough to serve as forms for a curved slab. With a circular saw, cut strips about 4 inches wide with the outer grain running lengthwise. Then set the saw for a depth of $\frac{1}{2}$ inch and saw across the strip. Check that the blade cuts through no more than three of the plywood's five layers. Adjust the saw as necessary, then cut grooves across the strip every inch or so.

PLYWOOD   LATH

2. Installing form boards.

◆ To measure for curved form boards, first cut a strip of lath 4 to 8 feet long. Tack it to support stakes, even with the tops and butted against the house.

◆ Mark the lath at the midpoint of the support stake nearest the end, then pry off the lath and transfer the mark to a strip of $\frac{3}{4}$-inch plywood cut as wide as the slab depth. Trim the plywood at the mark.

◆ Cut slots in the plywood to make it pliable *(opposite)*, then nail it to the support stakes.

◆ Proceed around the slab perimeter in this fashion, butting sections of plywood at support stakes *(inset)*.

◆ Install expansion-joint forms as necessary *(page 90)*.

3. Sloping the forms.

◆ Work around the curved form, lifting or hammering down the boards and stakes until the top edge of the form just grazes the grading lines. Repeat for the straight forms of the expansion joints.

◆ When both the curved and the straight forms are adjusted, secure the support stakes with braces *(page 91)*.

◆ Correct the depth of the excavation to match the slope of the grade, then spread a gravel drainage bed 4 inches thick.

◆ Install joint filler as shown on page 92.

4. Cutting mesh to fit the form.

◆ Unroll a length of wire mesh over a section of the form, letting it overlap the curve of the form boards where necessary.

◆ Anchor the mesh temporarily with cinder blocks, then cut the mesh along the curve, 2 inches inside the form.

◆ Flatten the mesh either by bending or by removing it from the form and walking it flat.

◆ Cut additional sections of mesh, allowing each to overlap the previous section by 6 inches. Flatten the sections and tie them together with binding wire.

Pouring and Finishing Concrete

The key requirement for pouring and finishing a concrete slab is speed. On a dry, windy day, it may take only three hours for freshly poured concrete to become too stiff to work. For a 10-by-12 slab, two people will need about an hour for the heavy work of pouring, leveling, and smoothing the concrete, plus up to three hours to finish the surface. Until you have some experience, it's best to pour concrete in sections no larger than 120 square feet.

Mixing Your Own: A good source of concrete is a ready-mix company specializing in small loads—unless the slab is far from the street. In that case, haul the concrete in a rented trailer and mixer.

When making concrete yourself, test the mixture's consistency frequently *(below)*. Between checks, add water sparingly—1 cup per cubic foot of concrete at a time.

Planning for the Finish: Smooth and textured finishes to concrete *(pages 98-99)* need no advance preparation, but surfacing with oth-er materials requires forethought. For example, if you intend to apply a pebble-aggregate surface *(page 100)*, you will need a stiffer-than-average concrete mix. Furthermore, you must thoroughly wet the pebbles before pouring the concrete. Order $\frac{1}{3}$ cubic yard of gravel for every 100 square feet of slab.

Redwood rounds *(page 99)*, which are suitable only in dry climates, must be in place before concrete is poured. Positioning them requires cutting openings for them in the slab's mesh reinforcement.

The Process of Curing: After a slab is finished, it must be cured—kept moist and warm for at least a week to allow for the gradual chemical reactions that give concrete its full structural strength. The most common method of curing is to cover the slab with a polyethylene sheet. Colored slabs and pebble-aggregate surfaces are air-cured, however—left uncovered and sprinkled several times a day with water. Wait until the slab has cured to remove the outside forms.

TOOLS

Concrete mixer	Mason's trowel
Shovel	Edger
Rake	Hand float
Spade	Rectangular trowel
2-by-4 screed	Convex jointer
Bull float	Darby
Ladder	

Concrete Checklist

✔ When ordering concrete, tell the ready-mix company the dimensions of your slab and whether you intend to apply a pebble-aggregate surface or wish to have it colored.

✔ If you live in an area subject to freezes and thaws, make sure that an air-entraining agent—a chemical that creates tiny air bubbles in the concrete to prevent cracking—is added to the mix.

✔ Make arrangements for the ready-mix truck to arrive early; concrete sets more slowly in the cool of the morning.

✔ Have the truck park on the street, then lay a path of planks for carrying the concrete to the slab in wheelbarrows.

✔ Transport approximately 1 cubic foot (150 pounds) in a wheelbarrow at a time.

TRICKS OF THE TRADE

Perfect Concrete

Mixing the correct amount of water into concrete is crucial: Too little and a smooth finish on the concrete will be difficult to attain, too much and the material will lack strength and durability. The concrete in the left photograph above, although appearing somewhat dry, is actually just right; light troweling produces a smooth surface. A dash or two more water produces a mudlike mixture that is too wet for use *(above, right)*.

FILLING THE FORMS

1. Adding the concrete.

◆ Support the wire mesh on bricks, and oil the form boards to prevent sticking.

◆ Dump enough concrete into the first form to overfill by $\frac{1}{2}$ inch a 3- to 4-foot-wide section between the form boards, packing each load against the preceding one with a shovel. Use the shovel after each load to push the concrete into form corners and against the joint filler.

◆ Work a flat spade between the forms and the concrete to force the stones in the mix away from the sides. Then jab the spade vertically into the concrete throughout the section, to eliminate air pockets.

◆ If the wire reinforcement sags into the gravel base under the concrete's weight, hook it with a rake and lift it to the middle of the concrete.

2. Screeding the concrete.

◆ As each 3- to 4-foot section is filled, set a screed—a straight 2-by-4, cut 2 feet wider than the width of the form—on edge across the form boards. With the aid of a helper, lift and lower the screed in a chopping motion to force the aggregate down into the concrete.

◆ Then, starting at one end of the filled section, pull the screed across the surface of the concrete, simultaneously sliding it from side to side in a sawlike motion. Tilt the screed toward you as you pull it, so that the bottom of the board acts as a cutting edge.

◆ To level any remaining low spots or bumps, pull the screed across the concrete again, tilting it away from you. In areas around obstacles such as steps or window wells, use a short screed, cut to fit the space.

◆ Fill and level the rest of the form in successive 3- to 4-foot sections.

3. Bull-floating the surface.

◆ To compact and smooth the concrete, first push the float forward, tilting the front edge of the blade upward. Then draw it back, keeping the blade flat against the surface.

◆ Shovel fresh concrete into any remaining depressions. To reach areas beyond arm's length, bridge the wet concrete with a ladder supported on concrete blocks.

◆ Bull-float the surface again.

4. Edging the concrete.

◆ When the concrete is firm enough to hold its shape, run a mason's trowel between the form boards and the outside edge of the slab to separate the top inch of concrete from the wood *(right)*.

◆ Push an edger back and forth along the slot *(far right)*, tilting the leading edge of the tool slightly upward to avoid gouging the concrete. Any deep indentations will be difficult to fill during later finishing steps.

◆ Wait for any surface water to evaporate from the slab before applying the finish.

FINISHING THE SURFACE

TROWEL

FLOAT

Troweling a smooth finish.

◆ Place a pair of knee boards—1- by 2-foot pieces of $\frac{3}{8}$-inch plywood with 2-by-2 handles nailed at the ends—on the slab. Kneeling on the boards, smooth the concrete with a hand float, holding it flat and sweeping it in overlapping arcs across the surface. Then sweep a rectangular steel trowel, held flat, across the same area. Similarly float and trowel the rest of the slab, moving the knee boards as necessary. *(The concrete will be firm enough to walk on at this stage.)*

◆ After floating and troweling, go over the slab again with the trowel alone, this time tilting the tool slightly. Work the surface until no concrete collects on the trowel and the blade makes a ringing sound indicating that the concrete is too firm to work any further.

◆ Run the edger between the form boards and the edges of the slab *(above)* to restore edging lines.

Brooming a skidproof surface.

Hand-float the concrete and trowel it once *(above)*. Instead of the final troweling, draw a damp, stiff-bristled utility brush across the surface. Either score straight lines at right angles to the forms or move the broom in arcs to produce a curved pattern. If the broom picks up small lumps of concrete, hose down the bristles to clean them; give the slab a few more minutes' drying time before you continue. If you have to press hard to score the concrete, work fast; the concrete will soon be too firm to take a finish.

CONVEX JOINTER

Creating a flagstone effect.

◆ Immediately after bull-floating the concrete *(page 97)*, score the surface with irregularly spaced grooves, $\frac{1}{2}$- to $\frac{3}{4}$-inch deep, using a convex jointer. Place a ladder across forms as a bridge to reach inaccessible spots.

◆ After surface water has evaporated, hand-float and trowel the surface, then retool the grooves to restore the flagstone pattern to its original clarity.

◆ Brush out the grooves with a dry paintbrush to remove any remaining loose bits of concrete.

COMBINING REDWOOD WITH CONCRETE

1. Installing redwood rounds.

◆ Arrange 4-inch-thick redwood rounds directly on the gravel bed. Cover the top of each round with a sheet of 4-mil polyethylene, fastened with staples; then pour or shovel concrete carefully around each round.

◆ Level the concrete with a 2-by-4 screed cut short enough to fit between the rounds. Smooth the surface with a darby *(above)* instead of a bull float. Hold the darby flat, and move it sideways in a sawing motion to cut off bumps and fill in holes. Run the darby over the slab a second time, sweeping it over the surface in broad arcs.

2. Finishing the edges.

◆ When the concrete is firm enough to hold its shape, run the pointed end of a mason's trowel around the outside of each round to cut a V-shaped groove, $\frac{1}{4}$ inch deep.

◆ Finish the slab with a hand float and a trowel as on page 98. When the concrete has cured, remove the polyethylene covers.

PEBBLES FOR A TOPCOAT

1. Preparing the surface.
◆ Fill the form with concrete as on page 97, Step 1, but pack it even with the tops of the boards rather than above them.
◆ Level the concrete with a screed notched at each end so that its bottom edge rides $\frac{1}{2}$ inch below the tops of the form boards, then bull-float the surface.
◆ Scatter the damp pebbles evenly over the concrete with a shovel. Cover the surface with a single layer of stones, using a ladder bridge, if necessary, to reach inner areas.

2. Embedding the aggregate.
Tap the stones into the concrete with a bull float, forcing them just below the surface. After you have gone over the entire slab with the bull float, press down any stones that are still visible with a hand float, using a ladder bridge, if needed, to reach the interior of the slab. Then run the hand float across the surface as on page 98, covering the stones with a thin, smooth layer of concrete.

3. Exposing the aggregate.
◆ After surface water has evaporated and the concrete is firm enough to resist indentation, brush the surface lightly with a stiff nylon broom to expose the tops of the stones.
◆ While a helper sprays the slab with water, brush it again, uncovering between a quarter and a half of the stones' circumference. If you dislodge any stones, stop brushing and wait until the concrete is a bit firmer before continuing. If the concrete is difficult to wash off, work quickly to expose the aggregate before the surface becomes too stiff.
◆ After exposing the stones, continue to spray the surface until there is no noticeable cement film left on the aggregate. Scrub individual spots missed in the general wash with a scrub brush and a pail of water.
◆ Two to four hours after exposing the aggregate, wash and lightly brush the surface again to remove any cloudy residue from the stones.

A Curved Bench beside a Free-Form Patio

A wood bench is a handsome addendum to any patio, brick or concrete. The design shown here—for a bench shaped to a curved patio—is easily adapted to a rectangular one.

Choose a wood that is sufficiently resistant to decay and insects to be used outdoors. Pressure-treated pine is the least expensive but has a tendency to warp. Cedar, cypress, and redwood stand up well. Left untreated, they weather to a soft, attractive gray.

1. Anchoring posts.
◆ Use a 3-foot length of lath as a guide for chalking posthole marks on the edge of the patio *(right)*. Dig a hole about 7 inches wide, 11 inches long, and 1 foot deep centered on each mark.
◆ Cut a 3-foot-long 4-by-4 post for each hole, and anchor the posts in concrete. Let the concrete set for 48 hours.
◆ With a water level *(page 23),* mark each post $15\frac{1}{2}$ inches above ground level and trim them to that height.

2. Installing crosspieces.
◆ Cut two $3\frac{1}{2}$-inch by 1-inch notches in the top of each post.
◆ For each notch, cut a 2-by-4 crosspiece, $17\frac{3}{4}$ inches long. Center the crosspieces in the notches and nail them in place with $2\frac{1}{2}$-inch galvanized nails.
◆ Drill two $\frac{3}{8}$-inch holes, diagonally spaced, through the braces and posts. Fasten the crosspieces with 5-inch galvanized carriage bolts—or use brass ones from a marine-supply store.

CROSSPIECES

SPACER

CAP

3. Making the seat.
◆ Cut fifteen 1-by-2 slats long enough—at least 7 feet—to overhang the endmost crosspieces. Rip several $\frac{3}{8}$-inch strips from a 2-by-4, and cut them into 5-inch spacers, 42 in all.
◆ Position a slat so that it extends beyond the ends of the crosspieces by about $\frac{1}{4}$ inch *(left),* and nail it, edge up, to the crosspieces with 3-inch galvanized finishing nails, beginning at the center post. Next, set a spacer on each post, next to the slat. You need not nail the spacers.
◆ Alternate the slats with spacers to cover the crosspieces. Then, using a circular saw, cut off the ends of the slats parallel to the end crosspieces.
◆ Add 1-by-2 caps to the ends of the slats *(inset).* Fasten the caps to each slat with 2-inch brass or galvanized wood screws.
◆ Reinforce outside slats with a screw driven through them into the spacers behind them.

Brick or flagstone set in mortar can transform a drab concrete slab into an attractive focus for relaxing and entertaining. Unless you have recently poured a new slab, test it for soundness before proceeding *(page 16)*. Regardless of results—and no matter how new the concrete—use a metal straightedge to check the entire surface for high and low spots. Bricks and flagstones may rock on high spots and break loose. Water can collect in low spots and cause mortar to deteriorate.

Flatten high spots with a mason's rubbing brick or with a silicon carbide wheel in an electric drill. Break up low spots covering more than 1 square foot with a cold chisel and fill them as you would a hole *(pages 16-17)*.

Estimating Materials: Find the area of the slab. *(For a free-form slab, use the method shown on page 84.)* You will need $4\frac{1}{2}$ paving bricks to 1 square foot. For materials with nonstandard dimensions and for flagstones, consult a dealer. In either case, add about 5 percent for breakage and repair. Some flagstones are soft enough to be cut with a brickset; others are so hard that they must be scored with a masonry blade in a circular saw.

One cubic foot of mortar mix is enough to lay about 35 bricks or 12 square feet of flagstones. Buy additional mix to grout joints between bricks and flagstones.

Laying a Dry Run: Arranging the bricks or stones in a dry run is an essential first step. With bricks, orient the long sides with the slope of the slab. Doing so channels rainwater away from the house. Use a piece of $\frac{1}{2}$-inch plywood to space a row of bricks along two adjacent sides of the slab, trimming bricks as needed *(page 83)* to fill the rows. *(To lay a dry run on a free form, see the advice for tile on page 108.)* Leave the dry run in place as a guide for a string marker.

In a dry run of flagstones, vary the sizes of adjacent stones to avoid long joint lines. Spaces between stones should range from $\frac{1}{2}$ inch to 2 inches wide. Large gaps can be filled with pieces cut from stones that overlap *(page 104)*.

Expansion Joints: Always leave the expansion joint between the slab and the house uncovered. At the end of the job, after the mortar has set, press polyethylene rope into the joint, then cover the rope with self-leveling polysulfide or silicone caulk. If the slab is divided by expansion joints, matching joints are required when veneering with brick but not with flagstones, which can withstand expansion forces that can crack or loosen brick.

A Frame around the Patio: You may want to install edging around brick or flagstone to protect vulnerable corners and cover the sides of the patio. Set pressure-treated 2-by-8s or 2-by-10s in the ground on edge, even with the veneer surface. Metal edging is available for free-form slabs. An application of masonry sealant helps prevent the growth of moss and mildew, which can be unsightly and slippery.

TOOLS

Mason's rubbing brick	Rubber mallet
2-by-2 stakes	Mortar tub
Mason's cord	Hoe
Cold chisel	Mason's trowel
Brickset	Pointing trowel
Mason's hammer	$\frac{1}{2}$-inch joint filler
4-pound maul	Grout bag
	Wire brush

MATERIALS

Bricks or flagstones
Mortar mix
Chalk
Muriatic acid
Masonry sealant

Mortar and Grout

✔ Buy type M mortar, available premixed from building suppliers.

✔ Mix batches no larger than you can use in 10 to 15 minutes, about half a bag.

✔ Heap the dry ingredients in a wheelbarrow or mortar tub and make a depression in the center. Into the depression, gradually pour cold water as recommended by the manufacturer. Stir with a hoe.

✔ Mortar should be just wet enough to slide easily off the hoe. Grout should have the consistency of a thick milkshake. Both must be completely free of lumps.

✔ Before mixing a new batch, scrape or rinse all dried mortar out of the mortar tub.

✔ Moisten both the slab and the veneering materials before beginning work so they will not absorb water from your mortar and grout.

BRICK VENEER FOR A CONCRETE SLAB

1. Setting brick in mortar.

◆ Use a large mason's trowel to spread a $\frac{1}{2}$-inch layer of mortar on the rough face of the first brick in the dry run. Make a shallow groove in the mortar with the point of the trowel.

◆ Set the brick at the edge of the slab and tamp it firmly with the trowel handle to level it. Working one brick at a time, use the $\frac{1}{2}$-inch plywood spacer to position succeeding bricks. Level the bricks before proceeding.

◆ Stake a guide string to align bricks of the second course with the second brick of the dry run. Where a house wall prevents the use of a stake, tie the string to a brick and set it on a scrap of $\frac{1}{2}$-inch plywood.

◆ Level the bricks in each course, then reposition the guide string for the next.

◆ Wait at least 24 hours before proceeding to the next step.

STRING

PLYWOOD SPACER

SAFETY TIPS

Use leather-palmed gloves to protect your hands from rough edges of brick or stone. Irritants in mortar and grout call for a dust mask and gloves. Wear goggles when grinding or chipping at a slab, mixing mortar, cutting brick or stone, or when working with muriatic acid.

2. Grouting the joints.

◆ Fill a grout bag with a $\frac{1}{2}$-inch nozzle about two-thirds full and roll the top to squeeze grout into the gaps between bricks. With a $\frac{1}{2}$-inch joint filler, pack the grout into the gaps to a level slightly below the brick surfaces to make a drainage channel. Smooth the grout with the joint filler.

◆ Wait an hour, then remove ragged bits of grout with the trowel. Three hours later, smooth the joints with a wire brush, and hose the patio clean.

◆ Allow the grout to cure for several days. Then remove any grout stains on the bricks with a mild solution of muriatic acid and a wire brush. Hose away the residue.

GROUT BAG

JOINT FILLER

RANDOM SHAPES FROM FLAGSTONES

1. Laying out a dry run.
◆ Arrange the flagstones on the slab allowing $\frac{1}{2}$- to 2-inch gaps between adjacent stones. Ignore any expansion joints except the one adjacent to the house wall.

◆ Where a stone hangs over the edge of the slab, mark a cutting line on it with chalk, using the edge of the slab as a guide.

◆ Where stones overlap each other, mark one of the stones, allowing space for the mortar joint between them. Cutting lines should be straight; you can approximate a curve with several short cuts.

2. Cutting a stone.
◆ Remove marked stones one by one and score each for cutting. To do so, hold a brickset against the chalk line and tap it several times with a maul *(above, left);* then move the brickset along the line and tap again.

◆ For stones that are more than 1 inch thick, score a corresponding line on the other side by extending the first line down the edges of the stone and marking a connecting line on the back.

◆ Rest the stone on a board, with the scored line no more than $\frac{1}{4}$ inch beyond the edge. Then tap the overhang with the maul to snap it off *(above, right).* As each stone is cut, return it to its position on the slab.

3. Laying the stones in mortar.

◆ At a corner or along an edge, set a section of stones about 4 by 4 feet in area next to the slab as they were arranged in the dry run.

◆ Moisten the exposed slab with water, then trowel on a 1-inch-thick mortar bed.

◆ Position the stones on the mortar, seating them with a rubber mallet. Fill any large spaces with pieces of cut stone.

4. Making an even surface.

◆ Examine the flagstones just laid. If a stone sits too high, lift it aside and scoop out some of the mortar with a pointing trowel. If a stone is too low, add mortar and smooth it with the trowel to ensure a good bond.

◆ Finish each section by using a pointing trowel or a tongue depressor to remove any excess mortar that has pushed up between stones. Sponge stray mortar off the stones.

5. Grouting the joints.

◆ After the mortar has cured 24 to 48 hours, trowel grout into the joints. Then use a joint filler to compact the grout to a depth of $\frac{1}{16}$ inch below the stone surface.

◆ Wipe away excess grout with a wet rag within 10 minutes to prevent stains. Do not use muriatic acid; it may discolor flagstone.

◆ To ensure that the wide joints between flagstones cure adequately, mist the stonework with water every four hours for the first day, and allow the grout to cure three more days before walking on the patio.

The Many Possibilities of Tile

Hard-fired ceramic-clay tiles set in mortar on a concrete slab offer attractive, durable choices for outdoor patios or at poolside. Any outdoor tile must be frost-proof; purchase tile with an absorption rate of 6 percent or less.

Types of Tile: Quarry tiles have a smooth surface and come in squares, rectangles, hexagons, and octagons of various sizes. Paver tiles are thicker than quarry tiles and are commonly cast in squares and hexagons with a textured surface and rough or rounded edges.

Mosaic tiles, mounted for correct spacing on a 1- or 2-foot-square mesh backing, make fast work of intricate designs. For outdoor use, choose mosaic tiles with a matte glaze so the surface will not be slippery when it is wet.

Preliminary Steps: First, check the slab you intend to tile for flaws *(page 102)*. To estimate the number of tiles you need, calculate the area of the slab *(page 84)*, and purchase tile accordingly.

Laying a Dry Run: Note the position of expansion joints, if any, between sections of slab, and design your tile pattern around them *(page 108)*. Lay a dry run of tile to ensure accurate placement. Plastic spacers or lugs molded into the edges of tiles help position them precisely.

Cutting Tiles: You can cut quarry tiles with the hand tools shown on pages 109 and 110. Buy the micro-cutter and nippers; rent the more expensive senior cutter.

Tiles more than $\frac{1}{2}$-inch thick require a circular saw with a silicon carbide masonry blade *(page 83)* or an electric tub saw, in which water cools the blade and flushes away ceramic chips and dust. Regardless of the tool you use, always cut ribbed tiles across the ribs.

Latex-Base Mortar: A tiled patio lasts longer and requires less maintenance when the mortar for anchoring the tiles and the grout for filling joints between them are made with a latex tile-setting liquid instead of water. Ceramic-tile grout comes premixed in a variety of colors; a 10-pound bag is enough for about 10 square feet of paver or quarry tile, or 20 square feet of mosaic tile. You can make your own grout by mixing equal parts of Portland cement and fine masonry sand with enough latex liquid to make a thick paste.

When you are ready to lay tiles, dampen the slab and trowel on a thin bed of mortar. Set the tiles in small sections while the mortar is still soft, planning the work so that you do not disturb freshly laid tiles.

Allow the mortar to cure 24 hours before grouting the joints. Do the grouting within the next 24 hours, however, to ensure a solid bond to the mortar.

Preserving Your Patio: To protect tiles and grout from stains, you can seal the finished paving with commercial masonry sealer or a 5 percent silicone solution. You may prefer to seal only the grout, which usually is lighter and more absorbent than the tile and shows stains more readily.

 TOOLS

Tile cutters
Mortar tub
Mason's trowel
Notched trowel
Grout float
Caulking gun

 MATERIALS

Tile spacers
Mortar/grout mix
Latex tile-setting liquid
Polyethylene-foam rope
Silicone or polysulfide caulk
Masonry sealer

 SAFETY TIPS

When cutting tile, wear safety goggles and heavy work gloves to protect yourself against chips and sharp edges.

A typical tile.
Outdoor tiles like the textured example above commonly have ribbed backs to improve the bond between mortar and tile. Most tiles are available in a bullnose shape, rounded on one edge or two and used along the perimeter and at the corners of a patio.

A variety of shapes and colors.

The square tile above, perhaps the most familiar, is just one of many styles available. Six-sided tiles are best used alone *(right)*, but 8-sided tiles can be combined with small squares in an octagon-and-dot pattern *(below, middle row, left)*. Besides traditional terra cotta, tiles come in many colors and patterns, including a wood-grain finish *(above, far right)*.

COMPOSING PATTERNS WITH SHAPED TILES

Repeating a single shape.

Some patterns are inherent in the shapes of tiles. At far left is a stacked pattern of rectangular tiles—square ones are also suitable. At left is a honeycomb formed of hexagons; octagons may also be used.

Repeating two shapes.

The octagon-and-dot pattern *(right)* builds automatically with 8-inch octagons and 3-inch squares, or dots. A square-and-picket pattern *(far right)* builds from 8-inch squares surrounded by 3-by 11-inch pickets.

Patterns from many shapes.

Rectangular and square tiles, whose dimensions are multiples of the smallest unit, make a lively pattern with little cutting *(far left)*. The rubble pattern is achieved using broken paver tiles with their edges smoothed.

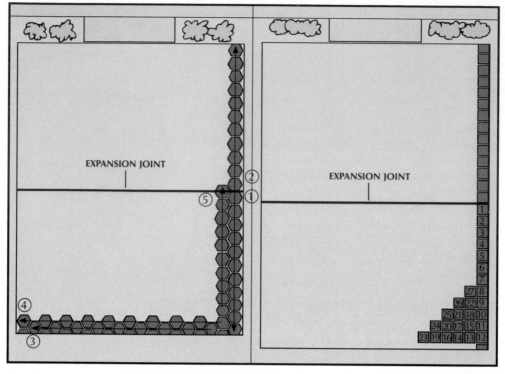

Rectangular slabs.

If there is an expansion joint, begin work there.

◆ For 6- or 8-sided tiles, set the first row to a far corner *(above left, Arrow 1)*, trimming a tile at the end of the row if necessary.
◆ Extend the row toward the house *(Arrow 2)*, leaving a gap at the joint; trim the corner tile as needed.

◆ Using the last full tile nearest the far corner as a guide, set a row of tiles perpendicular to the first, along the edge of the slab *(Arrow 3)*. Alternate tiles may have to be cut.
◆ Set succeeding rows *(Arrows 4 and 5)* in the same manner, letting some tiles bridge the expansion joint, until the entire slab is covered.
◆ Finally, cut tiles to fill in the gaps remaining around the edge.

◆ For square or rectangular tiles in a simple stack pattern, follow the numbers *(above, right)* to set the first row out to a far corner.
◆ There, use the last full tile as the apex of a triangle, and set tiles in diagonal rows until one section of the slab is covered, then proceed with the other section.
◆ Cut tiles to fill any gaps left around the edges.

Free-form slabs.

If the shape of the slab is irregular or curved, snap perpendicular chalk lines across its widest dimensions or use expansion joints to divide it into quadrants. Starting at the intersection near the center of the patio, lay tile along each axis toward the edges. Mark tiles for cutting as necessary. Then fill in each quadrant as shown above, right.

Interrupted slabs.

◆ To tile around a tree or pool, first lay a rectangular frame around the obstacle, then fill in the frame as necessary with tiles trimmed to fit. Add an edge of border tiles, if desired.

◆ Divide the slab into quadrants, using a tile at the midpoint of each side of the frame as a reference point.

◆ Lay rows of tiles along the quadrant lines, and fill in each section with parallel rows of tiles. Cut the outermost tile in each row to fit the edge of the slab.

FRAME

THREE TECHNIQUES FOR CUTTING TILES

SCORING WHEEL

FLANGE

ADJUSTABLE FENCE

CUTTER PLATE

BREAKING BAR

Using a senior cutter.

◆ Place a marked tile on the cutter plate, with the cutting line directly above the breaking bar. Set and lock the adjustable fence to hold the tile firmly in place.

◆ Slide the cutter handle toward you, then lift the handle until the scoring wheel rests on the line. Push the handle forward in one continuous motion, scoring the tile.

◆ Rest the flanges on the tile at its midpoint, then strike the handle sharply with your fist (*above*), causing the flanges to snap the tile over the breaking bar.

SCORING WHEEL

Using a microcutter.

◆ On the tile, draw a cutting line; it may be straight or gently curved. Set the scoring wheel on the line, hold the tile firm, and run the scoring wheel along the line in one continuous motion. For a straight cut, use a plywood scrap or uncut tile as a guide. Follow curves freehand. In either case, score the tile once; a second pass increases the chance of a ragged break.

◆ Center the jaws of the cutter on the scored line (*above*) and squeeze the cutter handles. The tile will snap along the scored line.

Cutting with tile nippers.

◆ Score a cutting line on the tile followed by a crosshatch pattern in the area to be cut away.

◆ Grasping the tile firmly in one hand, work from the edge toward the cutting line, chipping off small pieces. Hold the nippers with the jaws at an angle to the section of line you are approaching.

◆ When the rough cut is complete, smooth the edges with a piece of brick or a small stone.

LAYING TILES ON MORTAR

1. Applying the mortar bed.

◆ Set dry-run tiles next to the slab, then spray the concrete with water in the area to be tiled first.

◆ Working in sections of 3 square feet or so, spread a thin layer of mortar over the dampened slab with the smooth edge of a rectangular notched-blade trowel. Turn the trowel and draw the notched edge through the mortar, leaving a pattern of uniform ridges. Keep a pointing trowel nearby for removing excess mortar and scraping dripped mortar from the slab. Rinse both trowels often in a bucket of water, to remove mortar before it dries.

2. Laying the tiles.

◆ Hold a tile by its edges and lower it onto the mortar bed with as little sideways motion as possible. Tap the tile with a rubber mallet to seat it firmly.

◆ Unless your tiles are molded with spacer lugs, lay plastic spacers on the mortar at the corners of the tile, then place the second tile against the spacers.

◆ Lay all the full tiles, checking the tiled surface every 4 or 5 tiles for evenness. When laying interlocking tiles near an expansion joint, stand $\frac{3}{8}$-inch furniture dowels—available in bulk at hardware stores or home-improvement centers —between the tiles next to the joint (inset).

◆ Cut tiles for the edge of the slab as needed and mortar them in place.

◆ Allow the mortar to cure for 24 hours.

SPACER

EXPANSION JOINT

DOWEL

FILLING JOINTS WITH GROUT

1. Grouting the joints.
◆ If you used plastic spacers between tiles—and they are less than $\frac{1}{4}$ inch below the tiled surface—remove them.
◆ Extract any dowel spacers near an expansion joint and gently fill the gap with strips of rolled newspaper to keep it free of grout.
◆ Place small mounds of grout at intervals along the mortar joints over an area 3- or 4-feet square. Kneeling on a piece of plywood to distribute your weight and avoid dislodging tiles, force the grout between the tiles with a rubber grout float dampened with water. Dip the float in a bucket of water occasionally to keep it wet.

2. Cleaning the tiles.
◆ Let the grout dry for about 10 minutes, but not longer than specified by the manufacturer.
◆ Wipe away any excess grout with a damp sponge, using a light, circular motion. Rinse the sponge often in clean water, but wring it well to avoid saturating the grout or washing the pigment out of colored grout.
◆ Mist the tiled surface with water every 4 hours for the first day, to let the grout cure slowly. After the third day, remove hazy grout residue from the tile surface by buffing with a dry cloth.

3. Filling the expansion joint.
◆ After the grout has cured, remove the rolled newspaper from the expansion joint and press $\frac{3}{8}$-inch polyethylene-foam rope to the bottom of the gap (left, top).
◆ Fill any space remaining with silicone or polysulfide caulk (left, bottom), wiping excess caulk off the tiles immediately with the solvent recommended by the manufacturer. Let the caulk dry before walking on the tiles.
◆ If you intend to seal the tiles, wait a week or more to allow the grout to dry completely, then apply two coats of sealer.

Increasing the Comfort Quotient

Insects and the relentless sun can transform a deck, porch, or patio from paradise to purgatory. The solutions are tried and true. Shade, achieved in a variety of ways, lowers temperatures during the sultry days of summer, and screens keep out bugs. The arrangement shown for screening in a porch on the following pages is easily adapted to a deck or a patio.

Enclosing a porch with screens requires a suitable framework for attaching the mesh. If your porch has a knee wall—a partition approximately 3 feet high around the perimeter of the porch—and square posts no more than 5 feet apart, you may need to add only a doorframe and studs against the house wall at the ends of the porch. To keep flying insects out, notch the studs to match the siding *(opposite)*. Build the doorframe to fit the width of the door, but buy a door slightly taller than you need so it can be trimmed to fit.

Porches without knee walls vary in the amount of construction needed for screening. In addition to a doorframe, some may lack only a few uprights. Others may need a complete set of vertical and horizontal supports. Pick the elements that are appropriate for your porch from the ones shown on the following pages.

Attaching the Mesh: No matter what type of screening you choose *(page 8)*, there are a number of ways to attach it to the porch. The simplest is to staple the screen directly to the supporting structure and cover the seams with molding.

Or you can install screen-spline channels that fasten to the porch. The channels anchor the mesh with a flexible spline identical to that used in aluminum screens *(page 8)*. A decorative cover hides the spline and the screen edges.

A third option is wood-framed screens *(page 10)*. Although more expensive and time-consuming than the preceding methods, framed screens complement a large, elegant porch better than the others.

TOOLS

Crosscut or circular saw	Staple gun
Saber saw	Hammer
Compass	Utility knife
Chalk line	Belt sander
Miter box and backsaw	Drill
	Screwdriver
	Screen-spline roller

MATERIALS

2-by-4s	Galvanized common nails (3-inch)
Doorstop molding	
Screen bead	Galvanized finishing nails (2-inch)
Screen door	
Door hinges and latch	Screws
Screening	Copper-coated staples ($\frac{1}{4}$-inch)
Screen spline and molding	Brads ($\frac{3}{4}$-inch)
	Turn buttons

FRAMING ALTERNATIVES

A screened porch that stands alone.

The framework for enclosing a porch consists of 2-by-4 studs toenailed to the floor and ceiling. If you wish to attach screening to this supporting structure, space the studs no more than 5 feet apart, 3 feet if you plan wood-framed screens. Blocking between the studs at the floor and ceiling helps to keep the uprights from warping, while knee rails 3 feet above the floor help anchor the mesh.

A porch with decorative columns or posts *(right)* demands that the framework be recessed from the edges of the porch to accommodate doubled corner studs. If the porch has posts with flat surfaces *(inset)*, they can serve as the corner studs.

STUDS AND KNEE RAILS

1. Notching an end stud.

◆ To notch a stud for siding, place the face of the board against the house wall. Open a compass to the thickness of the siding, then move the metal point of the compass vertically down the siding so that the pencil transfers the siding profile to the stud (below). Cut out the profile with a saber saw.

◆ Snap a chalk line along the edges of the porch as a guide to installing studs, allowing for corner studs if you must add them.

◆ Nail the notched stud to the house with 3-inch galvanized nails set at 8-inch intervals, then install additional studs along the chalk lines, toenailing them to floor and ceiling.

2. The remaining studs and doorframe.

◆ Cut 2 jack studs the height of the doorway and nail them to full-length studs, called king studs (above). For a door at the front of the porch, the studs on both sides of the frame are equal in length. For a side door, they are different lengths to compensate for the drainage slope of the porch floor.

◆ Toenail the 2 stud assemblies, jack studs facing each other, to the floor and ceiling so that the distance between them is $\frac{1}{4}$ inch greater than the width of the door you plan to install.

◆ Measure and cut a 2-by-4 header to fit atop the jack studs. Fasten it with nails driven through each king stud into the header's ends.

3. Adding blocking and a knee rail.

Cut 2-by-4s to fit between the studs at the ceiling, at a height of about 3 feet, and at the floor. Between each pair of studs, nail one blocking board to the floor and another to the ceiling. End-nail the knee-rail pieces through the studs where possible; otherwise toe-nail them to the studs.

4. Installing stops for framed screens.

Molding nailed to all four sides of each porch opening prevents the frame from falling inward and positions the frame flush with the exterior face of the supporting structure.

◆ Rule a line around each opening as a guide to recessing the molding a distance equal to the thickness of the frame you will build.

◆ Cut pieces of doorstop molding—mitered ends result in the most craftsmanlike appearance—to fit along the sides, top, and bottom of each porch opening, then fasten the molding with a 2-inch galvanized finishing nail every 8 inches.

◆ Fasten a pair of turn buttons *(inset)* to both sides of each opening to hold the frame against the stops.

STAPLES

1. Stapling the screening.

◆ Cut a length of screening larger than the opening, and fasten the top of the piece to the porch with $\frac{1}{4}$-inch staples driven $\frac{1}{4}$ inch from the opening. Staple one top corner and then the other, restapling as needed to make sure that the top edge is taut and straight. Next, staple the rest of the upper edge at 2-inch intervals.

◆ Pull the screen down evenly over the opening and staple along the bottom at 2-inch intervals, beginning with the corners; then staple from the top to the bottom of the studs and across the knee rail.

◆ Cut away the excess screening $\frac{1}{4}$ inch outside the lines of staples.

2. Trimming with screen bead.

◆ Miter-cut 4 lengths of $\frac{5}{8}$-inch screen bead to cover the staples and to frame the opening flush with its edges. Nail the screen bead around the opening with $\frac{3}{4}$-inch brads every 6 inches. To prevent the bead from warping, alternate the brads from one edge of the bead to the other.

◆ Square-cut a length of bead to fit the knee rail and nail it in place.

SECURING THE MESH WITH SPLINE MOLDING

Unusual cuts at intersections.

◆ To install dual-channel screen-spline molding so that neither channel is blocked *(right)*, miter corners of the molding and its cover as shown for a wood frame on page 10.

◆ Where a stud crosses the knee rail, cut a 45° point on each piece of molding. The 4 points meet at the center of the intersection.

◆ At T intersections, cut a point on the molding piece that represents the up-right of the T and use it to mark a notch on the crosspiece *(inset)*.

◆ After screwing the molding to the frame, secure the mesh with a screen-spline roller *(page 8)* one opening at a time, first across the top, then at the bottom, and finally along the sides.

◆ Trim away the excess screening, and snap the spline cover into place *(far right)*.

SPLINE MOLDING

COVER

SPLINE

HANGING A WOOD-FRAMED SCREEN DOOR

1. Trimming the door to fit.

◆ With a helper, measure from the header to the porch floor on both sides of the doorframe. Then subtract $\frac{1}{4}$ inch from each measurement to give the door $\frac{1}{8}$-inch clearance, top and bottom.

◆ Transfer the results to the edges of the door, working from the top down.

◆ Connect the 2 marks *(inset)*, and trim the door to the line with a saw or, if the adjustment is too small for sawing, with a belt sander.

2. Hanging the door.

◆ Screw 2 hinges to the outer face of the door—1 foot from the top and 1 foot from the bottom. To ensure clearance between door and frame, tape $\frac{1}{8}$-inch-thick spacers above both hinges on the door's edge and on top of the door. Nickels, strips of corrugated cardboard, or $2\frac{1}{2}$-inch-long common nails work well as spacers.

◆ Have a helper hold the door in the frame so that the spacers touch the top and side of the frame. Shim the door to support it or use a block of wood and a pry bar as a foot lever *(left)*. On the doorframe, mark the holes for hinge screws.

◆ Set the door aside and drill pilot holes at the marks, then position the door in the opening and screw the hinges to the frame.

◆ Untape the spacers, and check the door's operation. Shave any edges that bind with a block plane or a wood rasp.

3. Installing a doorstop and latch.

To keep the door from closing too far, nail a band of molding to the doorframe.

◆ While a helper holds the door flush with the outside of the doorframe, mark a line on the frame along the top and sides of the door.

◆ Cut 3 strips of doorstop molding to fit along the top and sides of the frame. Miter the top molding and the upper ends of the side moldings; then cut the bottom ends of the side moldings square.

◆ With the door swung open, place the pieces along the guidelines drawn earlier, and nail them to the doorframe with 2-inch finishing nails set 8 inches apart *(inset)*.

◆ Finally, install a latch according to the manufacturer's directions.

Adding an overhead covering to a deck serves two purposes: It shields the outdoor living space from the sun, and it helps to integrate the deck with the architecture of the house. The covering can be a leafy bower, a simple arrangement of snow fencing unrolled on top of cleats, or a permanent structure of sun-filtering wooden louvers.

Building the Frame: The 8- by 10-foot frame illustrated on the following pages can be used to support these coverings and others. It will bear a moderate snow load of 20 pounds per square foot; if you live in an area of heavy snow, you should consult your local building department or a structural engineer for appropriate modifications.

Although the frame here is shown attached to a deck, you can adapt it for a concrete patio by se-curing the posts to the slab with post anchors and expansion shields. You can also build a covering if there is no underlying structure; in that case, the posts rest on concrete footings *(page 23)*.

In preparing to build the frame, buy posts somewhat longer than needed, so they can be cut to the right length once they are in place. You may also want to cut simple decorative ends on the beam and rafters, as shown on pages 121 and 122, before beginning construction.

Covering Options: The choice of covering depends largely on orientation and ventilation. If the deck or patio faces south and is heated by daylong sun, you may prefer a very dense covering for maximum shade. On the other hand, ventilation may be a concern; a solid cover attached to two or more house walls, for ex-ample, can trap hot air. In such a case, a more open covering would be a better choice. A deck or patio facing north is usually shaded by the house, so the covering can be chosen for its looks alone.

For decks with an eastern or western exposure, a covering that offers partial shade should be suffi-cient. A 24-inch eggcrate grid *(page 124)* gives moderate shade, espe-cially in the midmorning and midafternoon. For more shade, in-stall a checkerboard of 2-by-2 slats over the grid. Other choices for deep shade include snow fencing and fixed louvers.

In winter, a dense covering can keep warming sunlight from reach-ing the house. One solution to this problem is a covering that can be removed and stored. Another option is a deciduous vine *(page 125)*, which will lose its leaves in winter.

 TOOLS

Water level
Protractor or T bevel
Circular saw
Chalk line
Staple gun
Saber saw
Combination square
Nail set

 MATERIALS

Flashing
4-by-4 posts
2-by-6 or larger
   framing lumber
1-by-6 lumber
   for spacers
2-by-2 slats
Snow-fencing or
   woven-reed panels
Post-and-beam
   connectors

Joist hangers
Carriage bolts
   ($\frac{1}{2}$- by 6-inch)
Galvanized nails
   (2-inch and 3-inch)
Galvanized
   finishing nails
   ($2\frac{1}{2}$-inch and
   3-inch)
Copper staples
   ($\frac{1}{2}$-inch)

 SAFETY TIPS

Protect your eyes when hammering nails and when us-ing a circular saw. Earplugs reduce the noise of this tool to a safe level, and a dust mask is advisable when sawing pressure-treated lumber, which contains arsenic compounds as a preservative. Wash any exposed skin thoroughly after handling pressure-treated lumber.

Choosing Lumber of the Right Size

When building a framework over a deck, the standard post size is 4-by-4. Lumber for the beam and rafters varies in dimension, de-pending on the distances they span. Use the chart below to determine the correct lumber for your needs.

BEAM	
Distance between posts	**Beam size**
6 feet	two 2 x 6s
8 feet	two 2 x 8s

RAFTERS	
Distance between ledger and beam	**Rafter size**
10 feet	2 x 6
12 feet	2 x 8
16 feet	2 x 10

1. Securing the posts.
◆ Bolt a ledger board on the side of the house and add flashing *(page 39)*.
◆ On the outside edge of the deck, position two 4-by-4 posts flush with the bottom of the ribbon board, aligning the outer edges of the posts so that they are 2 inches in from the ends of the ledger; this leaves room to nail the outermost joist hangers to the ledger. Attach the posts to the ribbon board with 6 inch-long $\frac{1}{2}$-inch carriage bolts *(inset)*.
◆ With a helper, use a water level to mark each post at the height of the ledger's bottom edge. Then subtract the width of the beam lumber and cut the posts to that height.

2. Attaching the beam.
◆ Cut 2 boards for the beam, each 2 feet longer than the distance between posts to allow for an overhang on both sides.
◆ Nail the boards together at 16-inch intervals, using 3-inch galvanized nails and working from alternate sides of the assembly.
◆ Attach post-and-beam connectors to the top of each post and, with a helper, lift the assembled beam into them. Center the beam and nail it to the brackets.

3. Installing the rafters.

◆ Draw a vertical pencil line 2¾ inches in from each end of the ledger board to mark where the end rafters will be centered; this measure includes 2 inches for the joist hangers, plus half the thickness of the rafter.

◆ Subdivide the distance between the lines so that the interior rafters will be evenly spaced and no more than 2 feet apart. Center and nail a joist hanger over each mark.

◆ Mark corresponding lines on top of the beam, beginning ¾ inch in from the outer face of each post.

◆ Cut the rafters to length, allowing for a decorative overhang beyond the beam. Slip one end of each rafter into a joist hanger, and center the rafter over the corresponding line on the beam. Nail the rafter end to the joist hanger, then toenail the rafter to the beam using two 3-inch nails on each side.

◆ From the same size lumber you used for the rafters, cut blocking boards that will fit on top of the beam between the rafters to prevent them from twisting. Stagger the boards so you can end-nail them through the sides of the rafters.

SHADE FROM SLANTED LOUVERS

1. Cutting the spacers.

◆ With a protractor or a T bevel, mark a length of 1-by-4 lumber with parallel lines spaced 4 inches apart and angled to the desired slant of the louvers (box, right). Then cut along the lines with a circular saw.

◆ Nail spacers to the beam ends of a pair of rafters with 2-inch galvanized finishing nails. The spacers should extend only as far as the inner edge of the beam (inset).

Planning for Louvers

Shade provided by louvers depends mainly on two factors. One is the direction of the louvers. For decks with a southern exposure, louvers that slope down toward the house admit more sunlight, while louvers that slope up toward the house provide more shade. For an eastern exposure, downward-slanted louvers give the most sunlight in the morning; reversing the tilt offers more sun in the afternoon. The opposite holds for decks facing west.

The other consideration is louver angle. Although louvers are commonly angled between 40° and 50°, you may wish to calculate a louver angle that will capture maximum winter sun for your house. Find your latitude in an atlas. Round it to the nearest degree, and subtract it from 66° (the latitude of the Arctic Circle). Installing your louvers at the resulting angle will give you the greatest warmth in winter. This setting also blocks about 75 percent of solar radiation on the longest day of summer. To let in more summer sun, increase the louver angle; for less, decrease it.

2. Installing the louvers.

◆ Cut a 1-by-6 louver to fit between the two rafters, and nail it to the spacers with 3-inch nails. Place a second pair of spacers snugly against the louver and face-nail them to the rafters with 2-inch galvanized finishing nails. Attach a second louver to the spacers.

◆ Continue adding spacers and louvers until the entire row has been filled.

◆ Cut two filler-spacers shaped to fit between the last louver and the vertical face of the ledger, then nail them to the rafters.

◆ Add spacers and louvers between each pair of rafters in the same way *(inset).*

SUN SHIELDS OF WOVEN REEDS OR SNOW FENCING

1. Installing cleats.

◆ To support frames for woven-reed panels, nail 1-by-2 cleats along the lower edge of each rafter with 2-inch nails. Make the cleats long enough to extend from the inner face of the beam to the joist hanger.

◆ Build rectangular frames of 2-by-2s to rest securely on the cleats, but fit them loosely enough to be removed in winter. The frame pieces can simply be butt-nailed to each other at the corners with 3-inch nails.

2. Attaching the reed.

◆ Lay a roll of woven-reed fencing over a frame and fasten it in place *(above)* with $\frac{1}{2}$-inch copper-plated staples spaced 2 inches apart. Trim away all of the excess fencing with a saber saw. Repeat this procedure for each frame.

◆ Lower the frames into place on top of the cleats *(inset).*

◆ In windy areas, secure the frames with screw eyes set into the underside of the frames and screw hooks fastened into the cleats.

Shading with snow fencing.

◆ Install cleats in the same manner as for woven-reed panels *(page 123)*.

◆ Cut the fencing to fit between the rafters, leaving intact one of the two binding wires that hold the fence pickets together. Lay the trimmed fencing directly on top of the cleats.

◆ Nail a second set of 1-by-2 cleats on top of the fencing to hold it in place.

THE VERSATILITY OF ORDINARY LUMBER

Constructing an airy eggcrate.

◆ Beginning 2 feet from the ledger board, mark the bottoms of the end rafters at 2-foot intervals. Snap a chalk line between the pairs of marks to transfer the measurements to interior rafters. Then use a combination square to extend these marks to the vertical faces of each rafter.

◆ Cut crosspieces of rafter lumber to fit between the rafters.

◆ Nail the crosspieces between rafters at the marks with 3-inch galvanized finishing nails. Butt-nail the crosspieces through the sides of the rafters wherever possible, and use a nail set to sink nail heads into the rafter so they will not interfere with the installation of other crosspieces. Where butt-nailing is not possible, toenail the crosspieces to the rafters.

124

Adding a checkerboard grid.

For deeper shade, top each square of an eggcrate covering with eight 2-by-2 slats, each cut 24 inches long.

◆ Starting with a corner square at the ledger, place the first slat across 2 rafters so that its ends overlap half of each rafter and its inner edge overlaps half the ledger. Nail each end to a rafter with $2\frac{1}{2}$-inch galvanized finishing nails; make sure the nails do not angle back toward the ledger and pierce the flashing.

◆ Center the second slat between the rafters at the opposite end of the square, aligning its outer edge with the midpoint of the crosspiece. Nail its ends to the rafters.

◆ Fill the intervening area with 6 more slats, evenly spaced and nailed in the same manner. For less shade, use fewer, more widely spaced boards.

◆ On the adjacent squares, reverse the direction of the slats. To protect the top of the ledger flashing, face-nail a 2-by-2 nailing board to the ledger between the rafters. Nail the slats to the nailing board and the crosspiece.

◆ Continue in this fashion, alternating the direction of the slats on adjacent squares, to create a checkerboard pattern *(inset)*.

A LEAFY BOWER

Chosen and placed with care, a vine trained over an eggcrate covering, as shown at left, will control not only how much shade you get but when you get it.

There are many varieties to choose from. Some survive for years, but may develop slowly; others, such as morning glory or moonflower, grow as much as 25 feet in their single season of life, providing nearly instant cover.

Wisteria, grape, and other deciduous vines will cool a patio in summer; in the fall they will drop their leaves to let the winter sun reach the house. Evergreens, such as jasmine and Cape honeysuckle, will shelter decks and patios in southern climates all year long.

How much shade a vine will provide depends both on its growth habits and on its leaves. Vines that cling by means of hooks, thorns, or tendrils do not offer as much shade as those that twist densely around themselves and their supports. Vines with small, translucent leaves like those of the silver-lace simply filter the sunshine, while the large, opaque leaves of the English ivy or hop vine can overlap one another to blot out the sun.

Many vines have decorative fruits and flowers—but these can be a mixed blessing. Keep in mind that flowers, fruits, and berries tend to litter a deck or patio. They also attract bees and birds, a nuisance to some. And beware of some intriguing flowers, such as those of the Dutchman's pipe, which have an objectionable smell.

INDEX

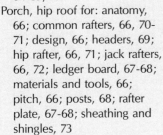

Time-Life Books is a division of Time Life Inc.

PRESIDENT and CEO: John M. Fahey, Jr.
EDITOR-IN-CHIEF: John L. Papanek

TIME-LIFE BOOKS

MANAGING EDITOR: Roberta Conlan

Executive Art Director: Ellen Robling
Director of Photography and Research:
  John Conrad Weiser
Senior Editors: Russell B. Adams, Jr., Dale
  M. Brown, Janet Cave, Lee Hassig,
  Robert Somerville, Henry Woodhead
Director of Technology: Eileen Bradley
Director of Editorial Operations: Prudence
  G. Harris
Library: Louise D. Forstall

PRESIDENT: John D. Hall

Vice President, Director of Marketing:
  Nancy K. Jones
*Vice President, New Product Develop-
  ment:* Neil Kagan
Vice President, Book Production: Marjann
  Caldwell
Production Manager: Marlene Zack

HOME REPAIR AND IMPROVEMENT

SERIES EDITOR: Lee Hassig
Administrative Editor: Barbara Levitt

Editorial Staff for *Decks, Porches, and
  Patios*
Senior Art Director: Christopher M. Register
Art Director: Kathleen D. Mallow
Picture Editor: Catherine Chase Tyson
Text Editors: Lee Hassig, Esther Ferington
Associate Editors/Research-Writing: Mark
  Galan, Mark G. Lazen
Assistant Art Director: Sue Pratt
Senior Copyeditors: Barbara Fairchild
  Quarmby, Juli Duncan
Picture Coordinator: Paige Henke
Editorial Assistants: Renée Wolfe, Amy S.
  Crutchfield

Special Contributors: Peter Pocock, Glen
  B. Ruh, Tony Wassell, Eric Weissman
  (text); Mel Ingber (overread and index).

Correspondents: Elisabeth Kraemer-Singh
  (Bonn), Christine Hinze (London),
  Christina Lieberman (New York), Maria
  Vincenza Aloisi (Paris), Ann Natanson
  (Rome).

PICTURE CREDITS

Illustrators: Cover and frontispieces: Tyrone
Taylor and Patrick Wilson/Totally Incorpo-
rated; James Anderson, Jack Arthur, Terry
Atkinson, George Bell, Frederic F. Bigio,
Laszlo Bodrogi, Roger Essley, Charles
Forsythe, Gerry Gallagher, William J. Hen-
nessy, Elsie J. Hennig, Walter Hilmers Jr.,
Fred Holz, John Jones, Al Kettler, Dick
Lee, John Martinez, John Massey, Joan
McGurren, Eduino J. Pereira, Ray Skibinski,
Snowden Associates, Inc.

Photographers: **Cover:** Larry Sherer, cour-
tesy Bowa Builders, Arlington, Va. **End pa-
pers:** Renée Comet. **7:** Larry Sherer. **19:**
Larry Sherer, courtesy Bowa Builders, Ar-
lington, Va. **26:** Fil Hunter. **27:** Renée
Comet. **67:** Renée Comet. **79:** Renée
Comet. **80:** Renée Comet. **91:** Rick Mc-
Cleary. **94:** Renée Comet. **96:** Rick Mc-
Cleary. **106-107:** Renée Comet. **113:**
Renée Comet. **125:** Pamela Harper.

ACKNOWLEDGMENTS

Les and Barbara Allison, Washington, D.C.;
Josh Baker, Bowa Builders, Arlington, Va.;
Geoff and Meg Dawson, Washington,
D.C.; Joan L. Gregory, Vienna, Va.; Reed
Harper, Summitville Fairfax Inc., Alexan-
dria, Va.; Ben Hoenich, Glen-Gery Brick,
Wyomissing, Pa.; Mary Levine, Tile Promo-
tion Board, Jupiter, Fla.; Scott and Dibby
Smith, Arlington, Va.

**Library of Congress
Cataloging-in-Publication Data**
Decks, porches, and patios / by the editors
of Time-Life Books.
p. cm. — (Home repair and improvement)
Rev. ed. of: Porches and patios / Time-Life
Books. ©1981.
Includes index.
ISBN 0-7835-3850-2.
1. Decks (Architecture, Domestic)—Maintenance and repair—Amateurs' manuals.
2. Porches—Maintenance and repair—Amateurs' manuals.
3. Patios—Maintenance and repair—Amateurs' manuals.
I. Time-Life Books. II. Time-Life Books.
Porches and patios.
III. Series.
TH4970.T55 1994
690'.184—dc20   94-13264